THE
SEVEN M...
OF THE
SOUL

Tim Addey

Published by

The Prometheus Trust

Dear Mischa,

I think you will enjoy

reading our latest pub.

Best wishes

Don and Monica

The Prometheus Trust

194 The Butts, Frome, Somerset BA11 4AG, UK.

A registered charity, number 299648.

The Seven Myths of the Soul

ISBN 1 898910 37 5

British Library Cataloguing-in-Publication Data.
A catalogue record for this book is
available from the British Library.

Cover by Phillip Bentley

Printed in England by Biddles Ltd, Guildford, Surrey,
England.

To my father

for his love, wisdom and patience

Contents

The
Seven Myths
of
the Soul

The soul descends into generation, after the manner of Kore;
She is scattered by generation, after the manner of Dionysus;
Like Prometheus and the Titans, she is bound to body.
She frees herself by exercising the strength of Heracles;
Gathers herself together through the help of Apollo
And the saviour Athene, by truly purifying philosophy;
And she elevates herself to the causes of her being with Demeter.

Acknowledgements

My thanks to my fellow students of philosophy for their suggestions and criticisms as various drafts of this book were produced: it goes without saying, however, that the errors still included are mine.   Thanks too, to Keith Dunn for the diagrams.

Colour Plates

The colour plates at the centre of the book are:
1 The rape of Persephone (Vergina tomb painting c.360 BC)
2 Dionysus and Ariadne (390 BC)
3 The Titans Atlas and Prometheus (550 BC)
4 Heracles initiated at Eleusis (360 BC)
5 Heracles given his robe of apotheosis by Deianeira (440 BC)
6 The "mourning" Athene, (460 BC)
7 Apollo riding upon a swan (380 BC)
8 Demeter initiates Triptolemos; Hecate stands behind (460 BC)

The Author

Tim Addey has been a student of philosophy, mythology, mysticism and world religions for thirty years. He has taught mythology at the Continuing Education Department of Bath University and has lectured at various institutions on Platonic philosophy. He is currently working on his second book *The Living Philosophy of Plato*. He lives with his wife and three daughters in Frome, Somerset.

INTRODUCTION

The purpose of this book is to introduce the non-specialist reader to the philosophical interpretation of myth, using as a starting point a passage from Damascius, a philosopher of late antiquity. Mythology is one of the great vehicles of wisdom, both human and divine, and has been especially valuable in delivering to us the subtleties of the ancient world-view across a dark age of ignorance and materialism. The great advantage of myth is that it has an attraction to those whose rational faculties are only partially developed - as proved by the way in which young children usually respond so readily to tales from mythology. Where the geometry of pyramids and stone monuments allows us an insight into the Egyptian wisdom, ancient Greek myths of Gods and heroes serve the same purpose, so that an echo of the ancients' *sophos* (wisdom) still reaches our straining ears.

When the Justinian edict closed the Academy of Plato in 529 C.E. the intellectual basis of European civilisation began to become obscured by the mists of anti-rational extremism which maintained its malignant grip on the west for over a thousand years. Even when the power of the Christian Church, obsessed by the need to extinguish any teaching which challenged its orthodoxy, was finally broken, its unloved and unlovely offspring - material atheism - arose to further cloud the almost forgotten vision of the beautiful truth nurtured by the wise men and women of antiquity. But from across the chasm of darkness spoke the voice of mythology, first to inspire the artists of the renaissance, and then to prompt a few thinkers to investigate the fractured remains of the texts which had survived that darkness: Ficino and Mirandola in renaissance Florence, Thomas Taylor in Eighteenth century England, and others began the task of recovering from the ruins of the ancients the wonderfully liberating doctrines they once taught in academy and sanctuary, in busy market place and shady grove.

At the heart of these doctrines is the idea that each individual is a soul, descended from Gods of transcendent beauty, goodness and power, and, therefore, destined to rejoin those Gods through the unfoldment of her own God-given faculties. In other words, humans are essentially spiritual beings immersed in body, and not corporeal beings with a fragile attachment to spirit. Plotinus, perhaps the first of the great philosophers to see how the new religion would obscure this joyful doctrine said[1] that the aim of philosophical striving was "not to be without sin, but to be as a God." This is the great truth told again and again in myth: Psyche is reunited to Cupid; Persephone rejoins her mother, Demeter; Heracles is raised to Olympus; Odysseus finds his true fatherland; Prometheus is released from his rock to take his place among the Olympians.

Centuries after men had forgotten, for example, the Platonic teaching of 'reminiscence', they still remembered a myth which enshrined the doctrine in story form. The theory of reminiscence is Plato's explanation of why we as human beings are able to recognise abstract, universal and spiritual truths, such as justice, beauty and goodness: it is because the soul once possessed this knowledge - seen in a vision as she travelled in procession with the Gods across the heavens - but forgotten when she descended into the world of matter; the soul's activities in arts and sciences enable her to remember it - the rediscovery of these truths being accompanied with the kind of delight that we experience when we meet an old friend. The Muses, who preside over the arts and sciences of man, were the daughters of Mnemosyne - literally 'Memory' - and Zeus, the Creative Divine Mind. It is clear, then, that this myth presents to the thoughtful hearer the message that our processes of art and science are dependent upon not only creative thought, but also upon the *memory* of our pre-terrestrial vision of the celestial realm.

Myths appeal to the unperverted intuitive faculty; they uplift the heart as well as the mind. Their morality, which superficially is dubious to say the least, is of a higher order than day to day activities - and this, somehow, the hearer of myths understands, without necessarily analyzing it. But just because we do not need our rational powers to be fully unfolded to appreciate myths, this does not mean that we cannot find even deeper meaning by reasoned thought and meditation upon them. This book is not - could not possibly be - a complete exposition of the myths outlined by Damascius, but is an attempt to lead the reader to an approach to mythology which will, with time, produce genuine insights into the nature of the Gods, the cosmos and especially the inner self. Whatever suggestions are made concerning the deeper significance of the myths in each of the chapters concerned with the seven myths of Damascius, I am certain that the reader will find even deeper meanings if he or she takes time to reflect upon them in the quietness of his or her soul.

The word myth, or mythos, (in Greek μυθος) means 'that which is delivered by word of mouth.' It may be related to *meezdo* (μηζω) 'to murmur' and, whether or not this is the case, we may assume that myths are those truths which require the intimate contact between speaker and listener by which the deepest and most subtle realities are transmitted from generation to generation.

But what of the author of the verse on the myths? Damascius was born, it is believed, around 460 C.E. and died sometime around 540. As a youth he went to Alexandria for his higher education; in the late 480's he moved to Athens and between these two great centres of pagan learning he studied rhetoric, mathematics, philosophy and astronomy. During these years Plato's Academy had been failing as a result of the problems caused first by Proclus' prolonged terminal illness and then by Marinus' long period of infirmity; after Marinus' death Isidorus became the head of the school, but finding it beyond his ability to revive, he returned to Alexandria. Damascius, who had moved from the discipline of rhetoric to that of philosophy during his time at Athens, either immediately succeeded Isidorus to the chair of the Academy, or succeeded a short-lived successor. The task of reorganising the Academy was begun by Damascius sometime between the years 500 and 520: Averil Cameron has suggested[2] that it was the success of Damascius and Olympiodorus in this revival of the ancient school that prompted Justinian's edict of closure in 529 C.E.

Damascius was the author of many philosophical works, mainly commentaries on Platonic dialogues, perhaps his finest surviving work being *On Principles*.

From the writings of Damascius, who was often called 'the inquisitive' by his followers, we can see that he stands squarely in the mainstream of the so-called neoplatonic tradition.[†]   In this tradition the mystical teaching of Orpheus, the poetical myth of Homer and Hesiod, the ethical and numerical teaching of Pythagoras, the perfect inner science of Plato together with its external development undertaken by Aristotle, as well as the oracular sayings of the Chaldeans, were synthesised and given both a rational and mystical re-expression by the golden chain of philosopher-mystics of whom Ammonius Saccas and Plotinus stand as initiators and Damascius, Olympiodorus and Simplicius the completers.

Due to the mutilated state in which the Commentaries of Damascius and Olympiodorus on the *Phædo* were found, wrapped together in one scroll, it has taken scholars some time to distinguish between the two sets of writings. The fullest translation of both these commentators is that of Westerink, in whose work, *The Greek Commentators on Plato's Phædo*,[3] is summarized what little is known of Damascius' life and writings.

[†]   The latter Platonists, such as Plotinus, Porphyry, Proclus, Damascius and Olympiodorus would have, I am sure, rejected the *neo* part of neoplatonism as they would have considered themselves simply Platonists, 'unpacking' the teaching of the divine Plato, without adding any new dogma to it.

A few words may be useful, too, on the Orphic presentation of Greek myth, since it is sufficiently different from the general presentation of the same basic myths to have earned itself the reputation of being a kind of mythological apocrypha. Thomas Taylor gives a fine survey of the mythological and historical accounts of Orpheus himself together with an exposition of his theological system;[4] in it he shows how these myths formed the basis of mystic ritual. Orpheus was said to be the founder and formulator of the rites of Dionysus, as well as the first worshipper of Apollo. The legend in which, having descended into Hades to attempt the recovery of his love (Eurydike) he was then torn apart by a party of women Bacchanites, confirms his identification with Dionysus who was himself torn apart (see chapter four). Damascius was clearly referring principally to the Orphic variations of the myths he outlines in his verse, and presumably considered that his immediate readership would be familiar with the rituals derived from them. Orpheus holds up each divinity like one might a cut diamond to the light, so that the light from many divinities floods into the vision of the God being beheld, just as the light derived from many facets of the diamond shine out through the one being examined by the eye. Our elementary understanding of the Gods can be advanced by linear thought and 'family trees', but at a certain point the lover of the Gods must leave this approach behind and follow Orpheus into the profundities of the Divine 'other' world, in which all Gods are in all Gods.

I should, perhaps, clarify a few points of terminology immediately, since modern usage of two or three crucial words has moved a considerable way from their original meaning. *Intellectual* is generally considered to mean that activity of the mind in which logical process is primary: I use the word in a far wider way which, indeed, includes the logical process but extends through intuition and beyond, to that point at which the knower and the known are one: intellect, is this sense, is *spirit* or Νους, Nous, and the words intellectual and spiritual are, therefore, virtually interchangable. I use the word *man* to mean the species, not the particular sex, except where the more limited usage is obviously implied. That said, I have tried to use the more neutral terms, such a human, humankind, and people, where this does not interfere with the poetic, in recognition of the fact that in recent times our civilisation has belittled the female principle, to the detriment of both men and women. I also usually refer to the soul as *she*, following the ancient mythological tradition which more often than not portrayed the soul as feminine. Finally I use the words *mystic* and *mystical* in their best sense, which, far from being vague and unscientific, actually implies a greater precision and clarity than is normal to human beings. The true mystic approaches levels of truth which embrace such profound paradoxes that ordinary language and even ordinary thought become inadequate to his or her task; but it is a sign of the best mystics that they will not recourse to the paradoxical mode until forced, by the subject matter of their meditations, so to do.

Notes

1. *Ennead* I, ii, 6.

2. *The Last Days of the Academy at Athens*, Proc. Cambridge Philol. Soc. 195, 1969, 7-29 (24-25).

3. *Commentary on the Phædo of Plato*, trans. Westerink, North Holland Press, 1976.

4. See *Hymns and Initiations*, The Prometheus Trust, Frome 1995.

Chapter One

An Outline of Platonic Philosophy

Hark, hark, the lark at heaven's gate sings

This book is an attempt to explore an observation by a Platonic philosopher of late antiquity; in order therefore, to make it accessible to the non-specialist reader, it is necessary to give an outline of the philosophy to which Damascius subscribed. That said, I do realise that some readers may find this chapter somewhat daunting: if you are so inclined, do skip over this chapter, since the structure of the seven myths carries an inherent truth which can be found without this outline. Perhaps, if the myths capture your imagination, you will return to this chapter in order to answer any questions which may arise.

In devoting one short chapter to such an outline I beg the forgiveness of my readers, for, in truth, the subject demands far more space than these few pages. However, if justice were to be done to the great philosophy of Orpheus, Pythagoras, Plato, Plotinus, Iamblichus, Proclus and Damascius - amongst many others - the exploration of the seven myths would be overwhelmed, and so this summary of what might be termed Platonic philosophy is offered with due warnings concerning the necessary simplifications it embraces. A less dogmatic and more fully argued survey of Platonic philosophy must await another volume.

But first let us step back and admire the vista of the country we are about to enter, to which end I can do no better than quote the heroic Thomas Taylor's opening to his General Introduction to his *Works of Plato*:[1]

'"Philosophy," says Hierocles, "is the purification and perfection of human life. It is the purification, indeed, from material irrationality, and the mortal body; but the perfection, in consequence of being the resumption of our proper felicity, and a reascent to the divine likeness. To effect these two is the province of *Virtue* and *Truth*; the former exterminating the immoderation of the passions; and the latter introducing the divine form to those who are naturally adapted to its reception."

'Of philosophy thus defined, which may be compared to a luminous pyramid, terminating in Deity, and having for its basis the rational soul of man and its spontaneous unperverted conceptions, - of this philosophy, august, magnificent, and divine, Plato may be justly called the primary leader and hierophant, through whom, like the mystic light in the inmost recesses of some sacred temple, it first shone forth with occult and venerable splendour. It may indeed be truly said of the whole of this philosophy, that it is the greatest good which man can participate: for if it purifies us from the defilements of the passions and assimilates us to Divinity, it confers on us the proper felicity of our nature. Hence it is easy to collect its pre-eminence to all other philosophies; to show that where they oppose it they are erroneous; that so far as they contain any thing scientific they are allied to it; and that at best they are but rivulets derived from this vast ocean of truth.'

He continues, that to "evince that the philosophy of Plato possesses this pre-eminence; that its dignity and sublimity are unrivalled; that it is the parent of all that ennobles man; and that it is founded on principles, which neither time can obliterate, nor sophistry subvert," was the primary design of his setting forth his introduction, and I would urge those who have not yet read it to do so.

Now to many modern seekers, the claim that "the whole of this philosophy . . . is the greatest good which man can participate" will seem ridiculous, for the scope of what is now considered philosophy is very limited, and its effect on its students shallow in the extreme. But the philosophy championed by Plato is not the clever juggling of mind crossword puzzles: *it is the yoga of enlightenment.* The word 'philosophy' means, in Greek, 'the love of wisdom' and this love, once ignited in the human breast, burns deeper and brighter than any merely mortal love: those who love Sophia, love an Immortal Goddess. The effect of 'falling in love' with another human being is hardly describable - it transforms the lover's apprehension of music, the fine arts, the landscape, the smallest things, the greatest things, and, of course, the self: but to fall in love with a Goddess is to experience the sunrise where before there was only the guttering of candles.

Plato attempts to explain the supremacy of this immortal love in several places, and in several ways. In the *Republic*,[2] after Socrates has told his allegory of the Cave - in which the material life of man is likened to being chained to a bench, with only flickering shadows playing before the eyes, but the end of philosophy being likened to the beholding of the Sun - a listener remarks that the man who has made his escape to the upper world would not willingly descend again to the cave, but would wish to spend his whole life in the rays of the sun: True, says Socrates, but in the republic each man must serve his fellows, and so the enlightened man would, indeed, return to his former prison, to encourage others to make the ascent to the upper world. In the *Banquet* (or *Symposium*), Socrates repeats the discourse of the priestess Diotima who had told him that the object of the discipline in which she was initiating him was the vision of the Beautiful Itself:[3]

> "What effect, think you, would the sight of beauty itself have upon a man, were he to see it pure and genuine . . . able to view that divine essence, the beautiful itself, in its own simplicity of form? Think you, said she, that the life of such a man would be contemptible or mean; of the man who always directed his eye toward the right object, who looked always at real beauty, and was conversant with it continually? Perceive you not, said she, that in beholding the beautiful with that eye, with which alone it is possible to behold it, thus, and thus only, could a man ever attain to generate, not the images or semblances of virtue . . . but virtue true, real, and substantial, from the converse and embraces of that which is real and true. Thus begetting true virtue, and bringing her up till she is grown mature, he would become a favourite of the Gods; and at length would be, if any man ever be, himself one of the immortals."

Such, then, is the aim of this philosophy. It has little to do with the dry and purposeless scepticism of what is wrongly termed 'rationalism', and neither has it much to do with the grovelling which is commonly mistaken for the religious spirit. This philosophy starts with the essential spiritual nature of the soul, which led the bard to write, "what a piece of work is man! How noble in reason! how infinite in faculty! in form, in moving, how express and admirable! in action how like an angel! in apprehension how like a god! the beauty of the world! the paragon of animals!" Our failings, according to the ancients, do not define us; rather we are defined by our origins in the heavens, and by our destiny, which is to regain our starry station. To the philosopher-mystics of the Greek world the striving of mortals towards the divine light was spirit calling to spirit, a goal attainable: "For the mortal who approaches the fire, will receive a light from divinity: and he who perseveres in prayer, without intermission, will be perfected by the rapid and blessed immortals."[4] This goal is not to be attained by ordinary disciplines or ordinary learning, but, as Plato says in his seventh epistle,[5] "For a thing of this kind† cannot be expressed by words like other disciplines, but by long familiarity, and living in conjunction with the thing itself, a light as it were leaping from a fire will on a sudden be enkindled in the soul, and there itself nourish itself."

But let us turn to the principles of Platonism, in this chapter in general and then, in chapter two, with especial

---

† Thomas Taylor remarks that Plato here means by *a thing of this kind,* true being, the proper object of intellect.

reference to the journey of the soul, outlined by the mythological key set out by Damascius.

In general, there are, I think, nine essential doctrines which the student of Platonic philosophy must become familiar:

1 The One

The first truth philosophy must acknowledge is that of The One. All things without exception participate in unity;[6] that which is most universal is most primary. Therefore the source of unity, The One, is the first of all principles. All things, too, seek goodness, and just as the source of unity, The One, is absolutely universal, so too is the source of all goodness, The Good: The One and the Good, then, are identical, and this Mighty God is the first of all things. Without The One all things would be infinite; for without participating in unity every thing would have to be made up of a multiplicity of parts, and in turn each of these parts would have to be made up of a multiplicity and so on *ad infinitum* - quite literally; and a multiplicity of infinites would prevent all thought, feeling, action and order; for all these things are dependent upon some kind of definition. Without the common goal of The Good, the universe would be a disorder of conflicting forces which would tear itself apart.

The Taoist, using the paradoxical mode, perhaps comes closest to the expression of this inexpressible:[7]

> "All-pervading, yet Tao may not be sought; subtle and impalpable, yet it cannot be overlooked. If it

be piled up, it will not be high; if it be overthrown, it will not be low; add to it and it will not increase; deduct from it and it will not be diminished; plane it, and it will not become thin; cut it, and it will not be injured; dig into it, and it will not be found deep; fill it and it will not become shallow. Shadowy and indistinct, it has no form. Indistinct and shadowy, its resources have no limit. Hidden and obscure, it reinforces all things out of formlessness. Penetrating and permeating everywhere, it never acts in vain. It stoops and rises with the hard and soft; it mounts and falls with the Yang and Yin."

But this One, itself alone, is so far beyond our comprehension that the only appropriate response to it is silence. Any attempt to describe it fails; and the more one tries to find attributes for The One in order to understand it, the more one diminishes understanding, since the thinker has, by this very act, fallen away from The One.[†]

The Absolute One is the very basis of our search for truth: but having made the simplest possible affirmation of this, we will pass on - knowing that the temple of the One is the whole of the universe, spirit and matter joined in the absolute order which speaks to us of the Ineffable.

[†] See Proclus' *Theology of Plato* II, x, (TTS vol. VIII, p.165): "And in thus determining I speak conformably to Plato, who thinks it proper to abide in negations, and to add nothing to *The One*. For whatever you add, you diminish *The One*, and afterwards evince that it is not *The One*, but that which is passive to [or participates] *The One*."

2 The Gods

All things when acting as causes first produce that which
is most like themselves, and finally produce that which is
least like themselves. Thus fire primarily produces heat,
which is most intense to its immediate locality; dogs
primarily produce puppies; cats primarily produce kittens:
what does God the One primarily produce? Clearly God
produces Gods, who are most like him in oneness and
goodness.

Of all the errors of the schools of thought in Europe
these last one and a half thousand years, the denial of the
Gods is the most critical: as the world is increasingly
westernised we lose sight of the fact that most men and
women in most ages would have agreed with Maximus
Tyrius when he said[8] "In such a mighty argumentation and
discord, you will see one accord and agreement in all the
earth, that there is one God, the king and father of all
things, and many gods, sons of God, ruling together with
him. This the Greek says, and the barbarian says, the
inhabitant of the interior, and he who dwells near the sea,
the wise and the unwise. And if you proceed as far as to
the utmost shores of the ocean, there also there are gods,
rising very near to some, and setting very near to others."

From the First Principle of things to the very last of
things there is an uninterrupted outflowing of The One;
without the uppermost emanations of God - the Gods - the
whole scheme becomes flawed and ugly - and where
people's minds have embraced such a scheme there has
been profound darkness. Those cultures, however, which

have been most conscious of the Gods are the very same whose arts and sciences have lighted the world and adorned mankind's history.

It is impossible for people to maintain the vacuum which arises in a world view in which there are no Gods between The One and humanity: what has happened in our society's long period of denial is that the vacuum has been filled by a belittled and personalised God during some of the period, and by an aggrandizement of humans for the rest of the period. Both erroneous answers are destructive of the true spirit of religion.

The philosopher may affirm three great truths concerning the Gods:[†]

Firstly, there *are* Gods.
Secondly, that the Gods providentially sustain all things.
Thirdly, the Gods are unaffected by man and by the cosmos.

The Gods themselves, being pure unities, are, like The One, beyond all knowing: however, whereas The One is utterly transcendent and is in every respect alone, the Gods

---

[†] These three truths are stated clearly by Plato in his tenth book of *Laws*, and investigated at some length. At 885b he writes: "He who believes that there are Gods, conformably to the laws, will never at any time voluntarily act in an impious manner, or speak illegally. But he who does so will suffer one of these three things: either he will not believe that there are Gods; or he will believe that there are, but that they take no care of human affairs; or, in the third place, he will believe that they are easily appeased by sacrifices and prayers."

may be said to have suspended from themselves the monads which begin the series of causes and effects which produce the universe. It is by these characteristic series that we, in some way, know the Gods - for each series is what it is because its leading deity is what he or she is. To quote Thomas Taylor's Introduction to the *Works of Plato*:[9] "From this principle of principles, in which all things causally subsist absorbed in superessential light and involved in unfathomable depths, we view a beauteous *progeny of principles*, all largely partaking of the ineffable, all stamped with the occult characters of deity, all possessing an overflowing fullness of good. From these dazzling summits, these ineffable blossoms, these divine propagations, we next see being, life, intellect, soul, nature, and body depending; monads suspended from unities, deified natures proceeding from deities. Each of these monads too, is the leader of a series which extends from itself to the last of things, and which while it proceeds from, at the same time abides in, and returns to its leader."

It is worth emphasizing that the Gods *as Gods* are unknowable but *as leaders of characteristic series* we come to know them and the truth they distribute to the universe: we will see in the main body of this book how their paradigmatic powers are the basis of our highest selves. The six choirs of Gods[10] of being, life, intellect, soul, nature and body, have various names -

Being is the gift of the Intelligible Gods;
Life is the gift of the Intelligible-Intellectual Gods;
Intellect is the gift of the Intellectual Gods;

Soul is the gift of the Psychical or Supermundane Gods;
Nature is the gift of the Liberated Gods;
Body is the gift of the Mundane Gods.

For many, brought up in a monotheistic culture, the rediscovery of the doctrine of the Gods has been a difficult experience; a common reaction of those who have understood the philosophical need for the Gods is to admit their reality, but then diminish it by treating them as aspects of The One rather than realities in their own right. This is a very poor half-way house, for it neither honours the Gods, nor The One. As Thomas Taylor says in a footnote to his translation of Sallust's *On the Gods and the World*:[11]

> "The reader must not suppose from this, that the gods are nothing more than so many attributes of the first cause; for if this were the case, the first god would be multitude, but *The One* must always be prior to *the many*. But the gods, though they are profoundly united with their ineffable cause, are at the same time *self-perfect* essences; for the first cause is prior to *self-perfection*. Hence as the first cause is superessential, all the gods, from their union through the summits or blossoms of their natures with this incomprehensible god, will be likewise superessential; in the same manner as trees from being rooted in the earth are all of them earthly in an eminent degree. And as in this instance the earth itself is essentially distinct from the trees which it contains, so the highest god is transcendently distinct from the multitude of gods which he ineffably comprehends."

It is one of theology's ironies that monotheism has a One God who is less than polytheism's One God, for in monotheism the reality of other Gods would diminish The One; but in polytheism the reality of other Gods adds, if such a thing is possible, to the majesty and magnificence of The One.

3 The Worlds

We can see, then, that there are distinct series suspended from the Gods which are productive of 'worlds' or conditions of being, each of which has its own characteristic order. The model of reality presented here is of the simplest possible, being based on the first true number, three, which allows the mind to grasp the relationships of truth:[12]

The first world is that of Being; its order is that of causes. Being, or pure 'isness' is, of course, distinct from existence which is merely one of the lowest manifestations of being. Being is the first because without being and causality nothing else could be; thus being is the most universal quality after unity. Wherever being predominates over other qualities there is stability; we may say, therefore, that pure being is absolutely stable.

The second world is that of Life; its order is that of ideas. Again we must distinguish between particular forms of life and life itself: mundane lives are the movement of particular existences - but pure life is the eternal dynamic expression of pure being. Life is the third most universal quality after unity and being. The stable causes of the world of being are given a dynamic procession in this world, streaming forth as luminous ideas or archetypes.

The third world is that of Intellect; its order is that of creation. Intellect is distinct from things which are intellectual, in the same way that being is distinct from existence and life is distinct from particular lives. Pure Intellect is united to Being through the eternally perfect medium of living Ideas: in the mundane world, when an intellectual being is united to an idea it is inspired to create some work of art, in order to give that idea expression. In the world of pure intellect, the one eternal act of creation takes place in order to give expression to Eternal Life.

These three worlds constitute the Intelligible (or 'Spiritual') World, which is, from this point of view, a tri-unity. The tri-unity of immutable causes, dynamic ideas and creative order produces spiritual substances - unchanging, eternal and perfect. But if the last of these spiritual worlds is creative, it is necessary that there should be some canvas, as it were, to receive the creation. Looking then to the perfect pattern of the three spiritual worlds, the Creator projects this as three further worlds, which we may call the projected, or objective worlds.

Starting with that which is most like the world of intellect and the spiritual worlds generally, *(fourthly) the Creator informs a world of soul*, in an order which is regulative and assimilative. The soul assimilates to herself all the ideas of the intelligible world and the expressions of them in the sensible world; she regulates the downward moving energy of intellect in her rulership of the lower orders. While intellect creates, soul acts. It is worth pointing out that in this order of soul are many kinds of souls, of which the human is but one.

The relationship of the world of intellect to that of soul is especially intimate: the human soul is often referred to as a 'partial intellect' because the ability to act in an assimilative and regulative way is dependant upon access to intellect (and through intellect, to the whole intelligible realm). From this point of view, although the world of soul is a projected one, it should be regarded as a 'spiritual' world - as one of its names, the *supermundane*, implies. Since the soul is directly informed by intellect its *essence* is spiritual and unitive, even if its *activity* is usually below the spiritual and, therefore, characterised by multiplicity.

After the fourth world of soul, comes *the fifth world of nature*, which reflects the world of Life: here the dynamic ideas of the world of Life are reflected in the forms[†] or types of nature which continually vivify the mundane world. The order of the world of nature is that of forms, and is distributive, separative and type-giving, since the dynamic potential of ideas is distributed into particular types.

[†] The word *form* has two distinct but related uses: in the Intelligible world form is an eternal and unchanging idea (often referred to as 'Platonic Form'); in the world of Nature form is a more limited thing - a reflection of the eternal intelligible form, but by virtue of its emplacement in the projected world a perpetual *morphe* or type which shapes material objects.

The final world is that of matter; it is a reflection of the
world of being, pure matter reflecting the stability of
being, and occultly holding all the effects of every order in
the same way that the world of being occultly holds all the
causes of every order. The order of this world might be
called the receptive order.

These final three worlds - the projected or objective - also
make up a tri-unity, being the whole sphere which the
Demiurge (sometimes called the second creator) produces
from his contemplation of the spiritual world;   the
effective combination of soul, nature and matter being the
embodying or mundane world or order.

The doctrine of the six worlds, each world with its
distinctive characteristics, is, I think, an essential key to
understanding how the universe is unfolded. Ultimately,
of course, there is only one world - 'reality' - and the
thinker should avoid the trap of isolating each world to the
point at which the one world loses its coherence.

4 The relationship between the spiritual and material realms

Many human errors arise when either of these two realms
is ignored: in the great scheme of the universe we must
affirm that both the spiritual realm and the material realm
are good and true expressions of the One and the Gods.
What is just as important is that we are able to see their
relationship.

Because the spiritual world is transcendently causal,
dynamic and creative *it is always the case that things*

spiritual act upon things material - and never things material upon things spiritual. There are no exceptions to this, and even the least thing in the spiritual realm maintains this relationship to things material. In the complexities of human life, bridging as it does both realms, this is often obscured; and given that the principal part of this book is an examination of how the soul is changed by her experiences in the mundane world, my assertion may require a little more defence. It may seem, at first glance, that the material of the mundane world is having a causal effect upon the soul, which is in essence spirit, but on more careful examination we can see that this is not so. The soul changes by her own internal powers, since it is these which allow her to reflect upon her experiences in the world and compare her inherent paradigm with the actuality of mundane life: if the material world changed the soul by its own powers then, since all human beings receive the same general mix of experiences, all humans beings would be uniformly progressing through the various phases of spirituality, and spiritual unfoldment would be as automatic as biological evolution. This, clearly, is not the case. *It is the interior reflection of the soul, freely willed, which propels her through the changes outlined in this book - the spiritual working upon the spiritual.*

The error of western thought since the closing of the Academies of Philosophy has been based upon two or three fundamental misunderstandings, of which the confusion between the causal power of spirit and matter is one. Once this principle was lost, it was inevitable that many people would believe that God was incomplete and affected by our actions; that the soul itself was directly subject to its own exterior faculties and even its body; and that interior abstractions in human arts could be explained solely by exterior influences. The especial emphasis upon the historical and *material* manifestation of Jesus as Christ, which, according to Christian theologians, sets the Christian story above older myths, and the Christian religion above older religions, is part of a vicious circle which has been partially responsible for the diminution of the world of spirit in people's minds, even though the Church Fathers thought that their doctrine would enlarge it.

Again, it would be an error to forget that these two worlds are in a real relationship because they are comprehended by *The One*: the philosopher must always think in terms of the spiritual world *and* the material world, rather than the spiritual *or* the material. Dualism has as many destructive side-effects as materialism.

5 Ideas

The spiritual world is self-sufficient and unchanging: as such it does not depend upon the projected world in any way, nor is there any quality of necessity inherent in its relationship with the projected world. The reason why the spiritual world produces the projected world is really the same as the reason why the Gods produce the spiritual world: it is because of an unenvying abundance that overflows like a mighty spring, irrigating the lower slopes with life-giving water.

In this case that which overflows into the projected world are forms or ideas - the dynamic and providential life-givers from the realm of spirit. As entirely spiritual entities, ideas possess completely the qualities of the spiritual world: they are unchanging and causal, eternal and dynamic; they are ordering and perfective. It is because *they* are immutable that the projected world is enabled to change without immediately losing its identity and beauty.

All particular forms which nature can unfold throughout all time are held occultly within the depths of the eternal ideas; Darwin's theory of evolution, including its recent refinements, is hopelessly in error while this first principle is denied, but becomes a beautiful exposition of the order of causal succession when viewed as stemming from the world of archetypal ideas. The Ideas of the spiritual world act upon the forms of the projected world - and never vice-versa - and for this reason Plato, when dealing with scientific enquiry into what really *is*, enjoins his auditors to fix their minds upon ideas, and ideas alone.[13]

Some misunderstanding arises in English because we commonly use the word 'idea' to mean human 'concept': in philosophy we must distinguish between the unchanging ideas of the spiritual world and these concepts which, being the productions of a spiritual-corporeal being, share some of the characteristics of each realm. Concepts enlarge and contract with experience and circumstance: ideas do not.

It is worth making another distinction here, too. The forms of ideas of the eternal realm have a counterpart in the types or forms in nature, *but they are not identical*: eternal forms are, as we have said, unchanging, but natural forms - being part of the projected world and partaking, to a certain degree, of the character of matter - have a certain mutability. I think one can see a certain hierarchy of these natural forms, so that those forms which are closest to actual manifestation are most affected by environment, while the more universal forms are least affected by the actuality of material expression. The form of horse, for example, could be said to be stable and relatively unchanging, but within the general form there are species of horses the forms of which are being evolved by natural (or artificial) selection.

As rational souls we know nothing *but* ideas: when we use our senses to gain knowledge, our minds continually filter out the matter which has, as it were, gathered around the idea to make it physically manifest. Those various theories which postulate that we only know sensory things mistake what is termed in philosophy 'the occasion' for the cause: when we come across a round object it is the occasion for us to recall to mind the idea of the circle, but it is not the cause of us possessing the idea.

It may seem, on first reading, that Plato despises the material world and the senses which humans use to contact it. This is not really so, but the impression arises, I think, because he saw that the spiritual core of most humans was being ignored, and that while it is easy for us to receive sensible data, it requires a greater effort of will, in our present condition at least, to discover abstract ideas. Furthermore, ideas are the greater good for a thing such as the soul (composed as it is of pure ideas). No one, placing themselves in the hands of an athletics trainer, would

expect him to spend much time on exhortations to walk -
since that is a skill already developed - but would expect
the trainer to exhort him to great feats of running,
jumping and throwing. So it is with Plato: his dialogues
exhort us to the greater task, as being the activity which
will bring us the Olympic crowns.

6 The perpetuity of the World

By 'the world' we mean the whole of the unfoldment of
the Demiurge - his abstract laws, as well as the whole of
the material universe.

Now there are few errors that can, in the long term, be
more damaging to the human spirit than that which is
centred on an 'end to the world'. Such a concept forces
the yielding up of the doctrine of the essential immortality
of the soul; it leads to a carelessness with regard to the
Cosmos - our whole environment; it belittles the power of
the Eternal Creator.

We must restate the nature of the eternal: it is
unchanging. If the Demiurge, the Creator God, is eternal
then he must produce a perpetual[†] offspring: for the act of
creation is not a thing which is itself within time. For
Gods are both eternal in essence and energy - and if a
God's energetic manifestation is creative, then the creation
is one that is not bounded by limitations of time. We see,

[†] There is a difference between the *eternal* and the *perpetual*:
the eternal is which is above (and exempt from) time; the perpetual
is that which is in time but which is never-ending.

of course, that the manifested *parts* of creation have an allotted sphere, which in some cases means an allotted time. But the *whole* is perpetual and continually generates its necessary parts. The Demiurge does not at one time produce the world and at another time not.

Religions which adopt the doctrine of 'the end of the world' necessarily have as their god some lower creator - what the Greeks called a dæmon - which is, in reality, a generator of parts. Such religions inevitably embrace a large element of fear, which is the greatest obstacle of all to the accomplishment of entelechy, or final perfection, in spiritual-corporeal beings. Wonder is man's greatest teacher, but fear his worst enemy.

Societies which spring from these religions are continually falling towards short-termism, no matter how high the individual members of that society aspire. Ecological pollution, bad art and architecture, continual swings to political extremes, and many other evils can be traced, in part at least, to the effects of the short-term outlook in human affairs. The concept of a co-equal with God (the Devil), as well as eternal damnation are further erroneous developments of a time-limited creator: its ultimate effect is to produce a throw-away society, because every individual and group of individuals seek to become as similar as is possible to the God they worship.

7 The Soul, and her purpose

If the Gods fill *all* things with the Good, it is necessary
that there should be no vacuum between Them and the
last of things: thus the whole of the universe is a gradual
series of entities each rank of which *a*) participates in that
which is above and causal to it, *b*) subsists in itself as an
integral part of the universe, and *c*) acts as principle and
distributor of good to that which is below it.

In the general scheme of the universe already outlined,
we can see that from the order of intellect arises the order
of soul: pure intellects relay the good of the Gods by
remaining in the spiritual world and projecting into the
three lower realms a paradigm of the Good. The ranks of
souls, however, in varying degrees, descend from the
spiritual into the natural and material realms in order to
revolve with things mundane so that the Good becomes
immanent within these realms (thus we can see soul as an
instrument of intellect). Of these varying ranks of souls,
some descend into the lower worlds only in image, some
in energy and some in essence. Each rank is an
indispensable instrument which distributes *whole* spiritual
ideas into the parts of the projected universe. If the parts
of the projected universe were informed only by parts
rather than wholes, the cohesion and harmony of the
cosmos would be destroyed. There is an analogy between
this and an animal's DNA code which is entirely present
to every particular cell in its body. Thus the cell has the
pattern of the whole in its essence, but acts as a particular
part in its energy: so it is with our souls, which hold the

whole spiritual idea (at least potentially) in thought, but actualise the idea upon the part of the universe in which it is centred.

Rational souls - that is souls which are at least spiritual in essence - can consciously and deliberately unite with ideas; in uniting with ideas they can contemplate real being; in this contemplation they are drawn into union with the intelligible Gods from whom being is suspended; and in the union with the intelligible Gods is to be found the mysterious sanctum of The One. Plotinus called the soul the last hypostatic principle and warned philosophers to look no lower for stable principles:[14] we may say, then, that the order of soul in general, and by implication our own souls, have this purpose: *To distribute the Divine Goodness in the projected universe by contemplating the intellectual and sympathising with nature.*

Every human soul can, by cathartic philosophy, rediscover the unmoving and ruling centre, where all the spinning radii of the projected universe meet. Thus Maximus Tyrius says: "But to what shall I compare the spectacles of a philosopher? to a clear dream by Jupiter, circularly borne along in all directions; in which, indeed, the body does not move, but the soul travels round the whole earth, from earth ascends to heaven, passes over every sea, flies through every region of the air, runs in conjunction with the sun, revolves with the moon, is carried round with the choir of the other stars, and nearly governs and arranges the universe, in conjunction with

Jupiter! O blessed journey, beautiful visions,[†] and true dreams!"

We will see in our examination of the seven myths of Damascius that the Greek view of man as hero-soul is one which demands from us a nobility which would not be possible were it not that the soul is a child of Zeus, the Creator God, and Hera his vivifying Queen; and through this lineage may trace her ancestry to Rhea, the flowing fountain-head of souls.

8 Reminiscence, Experience and Virtue

Let us now consider in what way man arrives at those ideas which allow him to 'nearly govern and arrange the universe in conjunction with Jupiter,' remembering that that which creates, creates first the closest image of itself, and creates last the furthest and least image of itself: in the six orders, that which is immediately after intellect is soul.

Philosophy teaches us that the soul, being an essentially intellectual entity, has *as her very structure* all the ideas which the Demiurge used and uses in the act of creation; for all ideas are implied in each idea and that creature which can attain to one idea can attain to them all.

But it is clear that we do not *fully* possess even a single idea, let alone them all: for our understanding is partial in every respect, so that at times we enter the light of an idea

---

[†] Thomas Taylor adds here, that the visions of a philosopher are in this case beautiful because he contemplates the intelligible world and its ineffable cause.

and at other times we fall away into a darkness of ignorance. And as ideas themselves are eternal and unchanging it is necessary that we admit ourselves to be that which changes in the relationship of man to ideas. If we are the changing partner in this relationship then it must be true that we draw closer to ideas by changing in the right way, and fall away by changing in the wrong way.

How are we to reconcile these two positions - the affirmation that the essential nature is intellectual, but the actual experience of partial knowledge (and, therefore, partial ignorance)? For taking either without the other we fall into error, either believing ourselves *to know* completely; or believing our knowledge to be limited to the relative for all time.

The divine Plato shows us in several places in his writings - in the *Meno*, the *Theætetus* and the *Phædo* for example - that knowledge is not external to the soul, but that the knowledge she possesses is but a forgotten memory. It is, he says, by discovering images of our inborn but half-remembered ideas through our contact with the manifestation of ideas at higher and higher levels, that our vision of these ideas is brought into perfect and permanent focus. Superficially we seem to know things only because we come into contact with something exterior to ourselves, but in reality such contact literally re-minds us of what we already possess.

This doctrine of reminiscence is truly a key to the restoration of philosophy to the modern world.

Following this doctrine, we must assert that, since the soul is essentially intellectual, that which leads to her recovery of her full intellect is that which leads to the recovery of her true self and station.

Let us always, then, affirm that the life of intellect is also the life of virtue in man's case: for the virtue of a horse is speed, that of a lion is strength; but that of a man is wisdom. However, Aeschylus says[15] that "this Zeus ever decrees - that man arrives at wisdom through suffering". Thus the attainment of full intellection and full virtue is from that experience of the projected world in which the soul, through identification with it, rediscovers her own inner nature where samsara (the manifested world) and nirvana (the unmanifested world) meet. The Lord Buddha's final words to his disciples are recorded as "Work out your own salvation with diligence" and the first evil to be avoided, he taught, is ignorance.

The life of virtue is perhaps best understood by considering the words the Greeks used for it, *arete*, which is sometime translated as 'excellence.' Further, the path to full excellence is one of successive development, as we will see in the suggested interpretation of the myth of the labours of Heracles (in chapter 6).

9 Incarnation and Karma

This is the doctrine that we, as individual souls, descend from a higher plane to the material; set up a procession of causes and effects; are, in some way, altered by these effects or, at least, altered by our union with the causes; and that this alteration in us leads to appropriate new experiences as befits an order ruled by divine justice.

Virtually every major religion teaches this 'migration of souls' and those that don't overtly support it clearly do by implication, or have vestiges of an original adherence to it: for example, in orthodox Christianity, in the New Testament passage that deals with the Transfiguration, Jesus asks his disciples who men say he is - and one of the answers is that he is Elijah returned to earth. Thus, it is clear that within the Jewish tradition the idea of re-incarnation into a fitting situation was current. There is no denial of this principle by the founder of Christianity.

All things that proceed also return: if this were not the case we would have to postulate a number of infinites. Our influence on every aspect of our environment - spiritual as well as physical - returns to us: in the order of cause, the return is *without* the interval of time; while in the order of material effects it is *with* the interval of time.

No other explanation of our experiences is reasonable, given the reality and nature of divine justice, which is absolute and perfect: other explanations necessarily remove a greater or lesser degree of responsibility from the individual, and thus diminish the nobility of the human soul. Plato continually refers to this idea of karma, which in the last book of the *Republic* is laid out in some detail - the souls passing into the mundane realms being called those who pass under the throne of Ananke (or Necessity.)

In summary we may say, then, that man has two goals: one is to live the mundane life in a virtuous way, so that in this realm, in the next realm, and in subsequent lives our situation is as close to the best as possible - and this through many lives of embodied soul. The second is to arrive at the purest contemplation, unmoved by external circumstances, so that we unite with The Good throughout perpetuity - and this through the one life of soul as soul. In the first we pay honour to the Goddesses of Fate, in the second, to the Goddess Providence. By both processes we play our part in the distribution of the good to all things.

As Socrates says, at the end of the *Republic* already referred to, "But if the company will be persuaded by me; considering the soul to be immortal, and able to bear all evil, and all good, we shall always persevere in the road which leads above; and shall by all means pursue justice in conjunction with prudence, in order that we may be friends both to ourselves, and to the Gods, both whilst we remain here, and when we shall receive its rewards, like victors assembled together; and we shall, both here, and in that journey of a thousand years which we have described, enjoy a happy life."

Notes

1. From volume I of *The Works of Plato* in five volumes, translated by Thomas Taylor and Floyer Sydenham; the Prometheus Trust, Frome, 1997.

2. *Republic* VII, 519d.

3. *Symposium* 211d.

4. From the Oracle of the Chaldeans, see page 44, *Oracles and Mysteries*; the Prometheus Trust, Frome, 1995.

5. At 341d.

6. For a fuller exposition of this doctrine, and its implications a good starting point is Proclus' *Elements of Theology* (The Prometheus Trust, Frome, 1994), especially relevant are the first six propositions. See, too, Damascius *On Principles*, the relevant passage of this being found in The Shrine of Wisdom magazine, issues 37-39, Autumn, 1928 to Spring 1929.

7. *The History of the Great Light*, Huai Nan Tsze, Shrine of Wisdom, 1960, Godalming.

8. Maximus Tyrius, Diss. I. See page 9, *The Dissertations of Maximus Tyrius*, The Prometheus Trust, Frome, 1994.

9. Page 39, TTS vol. IX.

10. For a clear exposition of these six orders of Gods, see page 247 of the third volume of *The Works of Plato*, The Prometheus Trust, 1996; Thomas Taylor's note on the *Parmenides* (no. 101).

11. To be found in *Collected Writings on the Gods and the World*, The Prometheus Trust, Frome, 1994. See page 5.

12. For a fuller explanation of the levels of being, see chapter 3 of *Proclus, Neo-Platonic Philosophy and Science*, L Siovanes, Yale UP, 1996. On page 125 of this work a table is presented which identifies the six worlds, together with the unity which encompasses them all.

13. To take one of many possible passages, see the *Phædo*, 65b ff.

14. See Plotinus *Ennead* V, 1.

15. Aeschylus *Agamemnon* 178.

Chapter Two

The Journey of the Soul
in Myth

Heaven's exile, straying from the orb of light

Let us consider now the path of the soul, and the conditions through which she must pass. In the *Timæus*[1] Plato has the Demiurge (the Creator of the projected universe) causing 'partial' or human souls to ascend as into a chariot (that is, into the first subtle body around which other, coarser, bodies will form) and showing these souls the nature of his creation and the Laws of Fate whereby his eternal intentions are carried out into the temporal world. In the *Phædrus* Plato describes the first trial of the soul, which is to journey with the Gods through the heavens, starting with the lowest realm of the celestial regions, and driving a two-horsed winged chariot up through the middle kingdom until the highest heaven is reached. This is the meadow in which pure being is conjoined with eternal life, and it is here that the vision of perfect beauty is gained. But the soul's horses are of a very mixed character and whereas the Gods' progress is smooth and untroubled, the charioteer of the soul has a hard time keeping his course, the horses pulling in different directions and causing the wings to be damaged. In this tumult, souls have only a moment to behold the beauty which resides in the light of the highest heaven. And now, with broken wings, the chariot and horses are hurled from the orb of light - the soul falls downwards until she is received by the terrestrial regions. The very lowest realms to which the soul may descend are part of the kingdom of Hades, the earthly entrance to which was called Avernus by the ancients, and which means 'without birds'; some commentators have taken this to mean that the area was literally without birds, but we can see from Plato's description of the soul's fall with damaged wings that we could equally well take Avernus to be that place to which unwinged souls ultimately fall.

Plato says that the nature of the first life which the soul makes for itself here is dependent upon how much of the momentary vision of heavenly beauty she is able to recall. Further lives are shaped by the extent to which she is able to exercise virtue within the context of the life chosen, according to the ruling of *Ananke,* or Necessity, under whose throne the souls moving into terrestrial manifestation must pass. The movement upwards and downwards between the terrestrial realms and those immediately 'above' it[†] are outlined in the myth of Er, in the last book of the *Republic.* Here the purifications that enable the soul to move onwards to her next life are

---

[†] The realm beyond this terrestrial one is not the heavenly home from which the soul began her journey, and to which she will, eventually, return - for this heaven is only to be reached by perfected souls who are no longer under the power of desire. The realm adjacent to the terrestrial holds both Tartarus, in which the ill-effects of our failings in this life are purged, and the natural heavens in which we, for a while, find rest and refreshment before again descending to continue our task of unfolding our soul's faculties.

described; here, too, the means by which the choice of the next incarnation is made and ratified are unfolded. Eventually, to return to the language of the *Phædrus*, the soul may gain mastery over the winged chariot and its horses by the unfoldment of her innate virtue, and join the divine procession, following her God to the banquet without mishap. The virtues, as we shall see in the chapter on Heracles, are not primarily outward and practical, but inward and theoretic: the outward life, the experiences of the mundane world, the tests of the hero-soul, are the starting points of the soul's reascent. They are, so to speak, the *particular* reminders of the *universal* forms within the soul. And the universal forms are the means by which the soul finds the single super-form of the Beautiful Herself, so that it is beheld - contemplated - not with a passing glance in the tumult of her first procession, but with an unwavering and god-like eye, which the soul after her exertions and trials will be able to open. As Diotima tells Socrates in the *Symposium*, "Whoever then is advanced thus far in the mysteries of Love by a right and regular progress of contemplation, approaching new to perfect intuition, suddenly he will discover, bursting into view, a beauty astonishingly admirable; that very beauty, to the gaining a sight of which the aim of all his preceding studies and labours had been directed: a beauty, whose peculiar characters are these: In the first place, it never had a beginning, nor will ever have an end, but always IS, and always flourishes in perfection, unsusceptible of growth or of decay."

But at the start of the journey, the soul is an innocent, knowing only the heavenly realms in which she has lived her childhood: the path of the soul is from this innocence, through various trials and initiations, to the full realisation of her true self, in which her essential innocence is reaffirmed.

This journey is one full of complexities, subtleties and puzzles: for this reason the wonderful medium of myth is, perhaps, our best means to come to an understanding of it. For only myth allows us the ability to hold truths together which, in normal terms, would seem to be contradictions. Towards the end of the reign of the old religion, the Emperor Julian, and his colleague Sallust, attempted to defend the mythological approach to theology and philosophy. Sallust, in his fine treatise, *On the Gods and the World*, says of myths:

> On what account then the ancients employed myths, is a question not unworthy our investigation. And this indeed is the first benefit arising from myths, that they excite us to investigation, and do not suffer our cogitative power to remain in indolent rest. It will not be difficult therefore to show that myths are divine, from those by whom they are employed: for they are used by poets inspired by divinity, by the best of philosophers, and by such as disclose initiatory rites. . . . . But you will ask why adulteries, thefts, paternal bonds, and other unworthy actions are celebrated in myths? Nor is this unworthy of admiration, that where there is an apparent absurdity, the soul immediately conceiving these discourses to be concealments, may understand that

the truth which they contain is to be involved in profound and occult silence.[†]

But are there 'rules' with which to interpret these absurdities? Over the course of the next seven chapters the reader may pick out a few; for example, the death of a God or a hero may indicate either that his or her powers are being directed downwards to a new level of being (see the previous chapter, section 3) or that the consciousness is actually being raised up to a new level of being. Another example is the subsuming of one principle by another, represented by the killing, consumption or rape of the subsumed principle by the higher. But in mythological symbolism a careful examination of the thing being used as a symbol is all important, and this, together with the symbolic names used for many of the actors within a myth must be our main guide.

One further extremely useful tool in our quest for meaning is that of what one might call comparative mythology; and here we have one outstanding thinker to whom we can turn. The great mythologist, Joseph Campbell, suggested that one can pick out a universal theme of soul progress in the myths of the world. His

---

[†] "In addition to what the philosopher has said in this chapter concerning the utility of myths," says Thomas Taylor, "we may observe farther, that myths when properly explained, call forth our unperverted conceptions of the gods; give a greater perfection to the divine part of our soul, through that ineffable sympathy which it possesses with more mystic concerns; heal the maladies of our phantasy, purify and illuminate its outward thoughts, and elevate it in conjunction with the rational soul to that which is divine."

book, *The Hero with a Thousand Faces*, takes this as its thesis, and in this most admirable survey, Campbell offers this diagram as a simple outline of the journey:[1]

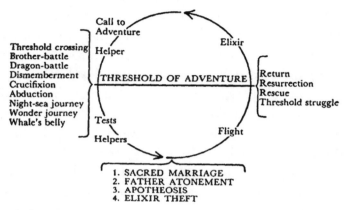

Figure 1 The Soul's path, from Campbell's *Hero with a Thousand Faces*.

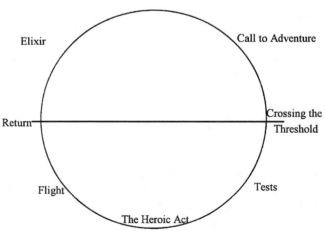

Figure 2 The seven stages of the soul's journey.

Leaving aside the 'meetings with helpers' which, I suggest, are the means whereby these steps are undertaken and can, in fact, occur at any point of the circle, we are left with seven stages (see figure 2, in which, too, I have reversed the direction of the circle, as it seems appropriate that we should represent the soul travelling in a sunwards direction):

i)   Call to adventure,
ii)   Crossing the threshold/dismemberment/etc,
iii)   Tests,
iv)   Sacred marriage/atonement/apotheosis/etc ('the
                                    prize' or 'heroic act'),
v)   Flight,
vi)   Return/resurrection/threshold struggle/etc,
vii)   Elixir,

which Campbell summarizes in the following passage:

> The mythological hero, setting forth from his common-day hut or castle, is lured, carried away, or else voluntarily proceeds, to the threshold of adventure. There he encounters a shadow presence that guards the passage. The hero may defeat or conciliate this power and go alive into the kingdom of the dark (brother-battle, dragon-battle; offering, charm), or be slain by the opponent and descend in death (dismemberment, crucifixion). Beyond the threshold, then, the hero journeys through a world of unfamiliar yet strangely intimate forces, some of which severely threaten him (tests), some of which give magical aid (helpers). When he arrives at the nadir of the mythological round, he undergoes a supreme ordeal and gains his reward. The triumph may be represented as the hero's sexual union with

the goddess-mother of the world (sacred marriage), his recognition by the father-creator (father atonement), his own divination (apotheosis), or again - if the powers have remained unfriendly to him - his theft of the boon he came to gain (bride-theft, fire-theft); intrinsically it is an expansion of consciousness and therewith of being (illumination, transfiguration, freedom). The final work is that of the return. If the powers have blessed the hero, he now sets forth under their protection (emissary); if not, he flees and is pursued (transformation flight, obstacle flight). At the return threshold the transcendental powers must remain behind; the hero re-emerges from the kingdom of dread (return, resurrection). The boon that he brings restores the world (elixir).

Now Campbell writes mainly from the point of view of the projected soul-ego rather than the pure spiritual soul; that is to say he sees the cycle starting in the mundane and going into the divine 'other' world before returning to the mundane with its protagonist transformed by the experience. This is, of course, a perfectly valid viewpoint and one that deserves the attention he gives it. The cycle analysis is, however, more universal than the particular application that Campbell unfolds: in fact any complete cycle through which the human soul passes - even a simple one of a day's waking experience - follows this universal pattern.

The present volume deals with the greatest cycle of experience - that of the soul's movement from first spiritual home, through its many incarnations in various realms, back to its spiritual essence - and thus the cycle we will unfold is, in some senses, the mirror image of Campbell's: here we start in the 'other' world and descend into the mundane, before returning to the divine world. We could, indeed, present a more complex diagram which incorporates both these circles, so that the larger cycle, that of the soul herself, is represented by a circle of greater diameter, while the lesser cycle, that of the ego-soul (or the conscious 'I') is represented by a smaller circle. In this diagram (figure 3) we see the soul in the mundane throwing off an 'experiencing self' (or ego) which rises out of the mundane, touches the spiritual world and then returns, as Campbell says, with a gift for the world; this advances the procession of the soul herself towards the permanent possession of spiritual enlightenment.

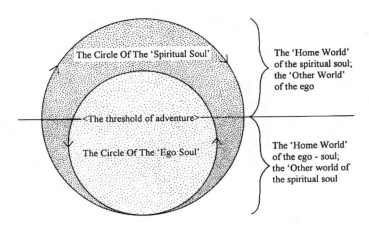

Figure 3 The circle of the ego-soul encompassed by the circle of the spiritual soul.

Having looked at Campbell's analysis of the seven phases of unfoldment, which was based on a broad survey of world mythology, we can now turn to a more ancient analysis which was based on a deep understanding of a single myth culture. Damascius' passage describing the soul's path gives us a remarkably similar picture to Campbell's, and this perhaps indicates that to reach the finest truths we have the choice of either embracing the multiplicity of the manifestation of truths, or of penetrating a single expression of them. Either method, if carefully followed, bears good fruit.

Damascius, in his *Commentary on the Phædo of Plato* (at I, 130) gives us this beautiful exposition of the soul's path:

The soul descends into generation, after the manner of
                                                              Kore;
She is scattered by generation, after the manner of
                                                              Dionysus;
Like Prometheus and the Titans, she is bound to body.
She frees herself by exercising the strength of Heracles;
Gathers herself together through the help of Apollo
And the saviour Athene, by truly purifying philosophy;
And she elevates herself to the causes of her being with
                                                              Demeter.

We can align these seven mythological figures (Kore, Dionysus, Prometheus, Heracles, Athene, Apollo and Demeter) with the seven stages of Campbell's analysis, so that we arrive at the following diagram (figure 4):

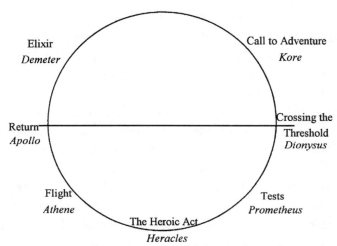

Figure 4 Campell's seven stages of the Soul's path correlated with Damascius' seven myths.

Since the verse mentions the key figures of the ancient mysteries - Demeter and Persephone (or Kore), Dionysus and Apollo - and since Damascius is commenting on a section of the *Phædo* which ends with Socrates saying:[1]

> And those who instituted the mysteries for us appear to have been by no means contemptible persons, but to have really signified formerly, in an obscure manner, *that whoever descended into Hades uninitiated, and without being a partaker of the mysteries, should be plunged into mire; but that whoever arrived there, purified and initiated, should dwell with the Gods* . . .

we might call our verse from Damascius his 'Key to the Mysteries' - in the recognition that one of the great mysteries of the universe is the nature and destiny of the soul. It is quite clear from the scraps of information we have recovered from ancient sources about the mystery cults of Greece that the central teaching of the initiatory rites was concerned with the immortality of the soul, and the path she takes. It is worth noting that in Plato's Academy the dialogue of the *First Alcibiades* was used as an introduction to the philosophical curriculum, and that this dialogue centres on the Delphic injunction "Know Thyself." Thus we can see that the relationship of the mysteries to the philosophy of the Platonists was, from its very outset, very close, and verging towards being merely two expressions of one overall aim - that of the yoga of enlightenment.

Much of the remainder of this book is concerned with the seven mythological figures named in Damascius' verse - Kore, Dionysus, Prometheus, Heracles, Athene, Apollo and Demeter. Each has a body of mythological tales which has survived to the present day (although it is clear that these myths were part of a much larger corpus), and it is my intention to explore the deeper meaning of Damascius' words through these myths. We turn then to the Greek mythological corpus, as far as it is known to us after so many years of neglect, with one or two cautions in mind.

Firstly, we must avoid approaching myths as if they were merely linear narratives. There are few in our society who have not come across the myths of the Greeks: it is a testament to their power, beauty and truthfulness that three thousand years (at least) after they were formulated, so many people - who, superficially at any rate, lead very different lives from those of our ancestors who first told these stories - still find the myths exciting and attractive.

Most westerners know the basic myths, but tend to have a rather simplistic view of them. Myth speaks to us of the great truths: the way in which the divine powers are related to each other; the diversity of the human experience which spans the material and spiritual worlds; the miraculous manifestation of divinity within the cosmos. Such themes really demand a more complex exposition than the simple style which, rightly, characterises our children's story books. Although the telling of the myths in Homer, by Orpheus in his Mystical hymns, and Hesiod's works provide the backbone of the Greek myth body, so to speak, the reality is that every age and every locality within the Greek-speaking world (and even beyond it) provided its own layer or its own perspective on the myths and their main characters. In archaic Greece, for example, the place of Ouranos and Gea was emphasized, while in Classical time the Olympian Gods were especially revered. In Dodona Zeus was especially connected with the might of the earth - his oracle spoke through the whisper of the oak leaves in the wind - while in the sanctuary of Olympia his anthropomorphic attributes were emphasized.

A detailed examination of the myth of the Greeks will reveal a kaleidoscope of patterns far removed from the simple linear stories most of us hold in our minds. Perhaps the best author to present this multi-layered, multi-facetted myth body is Karl Kerenyi: his books are certainly worth reading for those who wish to delve deeper into the myths outlined in this slim volume. In Kerenyi's

work one will find that every god and goddess, demigod
and hero, has more than one possible birth, sometimes
several possible parents, many different variations on their
main actions, and a whole range of symbols assigned to
them. One will also discover that every locality in the
Greek world had a different way of worshipping and
honouring the Gods. And this, of course, is as it should
be: even the simple scheme given in chapter one which
outlines the six Platonic choirs of the Gods is an over-
simplification, because each of the six 'levels' has sub-
divisions within it. Generally speaking, the further one
goes back in human history the closer one moves to an
understanding of the primeval Gods of Being and Life.
The closer one moves to 'civilised' times the closer one
moves to the lower choirs of Gods. Each of the tribes of
Greeks had their own perspective and expression of their
myths as diverse as their music, art and architecture.

My second caution is concerned with the nature of the
Gods and Goddesses themselves. Myths are clearly a
human invention - although, I would suggest, inspired by
divinity - and it would be easy to fall into the trap of
thinking that since the Gods and Goddesses are elements
of the myths, they, too, are human inventions: *nothing
could be further from the truth.* Sallust said of myths[4] "these
things never were, but always are" - that is to say, the
stories are inventions but the substance of them is
profound and never-changing truth; the reality of the
Eternal Gods ensure the timeless attraction of myth. I deal
with this important truth at greater length in the last
chapter.

Notes

1. *Timæus* 41d.

2. *The Hero with a Thousand Faces*, J Campbell, pub. Paladin, 1988, page 245.

3. *Phædo* 69c.

4. Sallust *On the Gods and the World* ch. 4. [TTS Vol. IV]

Chapter Three

Persephone

The soul descends into generation, after the manner of Kore.

The Myth[1]

Persephone is the daughter of Zeus and Demeter; she is also called Kore. In the beautiful Homeric hymn to Demeter, the start of her adventure is thus related:

> "She was playing with the deep-bosomed daughters of Okeanos and gathering flowers over a soft meadow, roses and crocuses and beautiful violets, irises also and hyacinths and the narcissus, which Earth made to grow at the will of Zeus and to please the Host of Many [Hades], to be a snare for the bloom-like girl — a marvellous, radiant flower. It was a thing of awe whether for deathless gods or mortal men to see: from its root grew a hundred blooms and it smelled most sweetly, so that all wide heaven above and the whole earth and the sea's salt swell laughed for joy. And the girl was amazed and reached out with both hands to take the lovely toy; but the wide-pathed earth yawned there in the plain of Nysa, and the lord, Host of Many, with his immortal horses sprang out upon her — the Son of Kronos, He who has many names.
>
> "He caught her up reluctant on his golden car and bare her away lamenting. Then she cried out shrilly with her voice, calling upon her father, the Son of Kronos [Zeus], who is most high and excellent. But no one either of the deathless gods or of mortal men heard her voice."

This scene is depicted in a tomb painting at Vergina (see plate 1) and although it is now faded, it still retains both a

beauty and an indication of the shocking loss of control
that Persephone suffers having once plucked the 'flower of
joy.' (Diodorus has the abduction taking place near Etna
in Scicily, where Persephone was brought up with her
fellow virgin Goddesses, Athene and Artemis.)

Thus was Persephone stolen away by Hades to become
Queen of the Underworld, with the active complicity of
her own father, Zeus. The echo of her cry finally carried
to her mother, Demeter, Goddess of Harvest, who began
a search of nine days during which she neither bathed or
ate. In some versions a fountain nymph, who had escaped
a similar fate through the intervention of Artemis, had
witnessed the abduction and tells Demeter. In most
versions, however, the searching mother is joined by
Hecate (herself identified with the underworld) bearing a
torch; the two Goddesses consult with Helios, he who as
Sun God sees all things on earth, and he tells Demeter
how, and by whom, her daughter has been stolen.

Demeter's grief turns to rage, and, disguising herself as an
old hag, moves among the world of men. She sits down
by a well where she is meet by the four daughters of the
royal house of Eleusis, and is invited by them to return
with them to their palace where a nurse for their baby
brother, Demophoon, is needed. Demeter takes the
position and during her time as the child's nurse
endeavours to give him immortality by putting him into
the ashes of the nursery's fire every night. The plan is
interrupted by the chancing of Mantaneria, the child's
mother, on the scene one night: she exclaims "My son
Demophoon, the strange woman is putting you into the
fire, I must mourn and lament for you." Demeter, her

disguise falling away, takes the child - not yet made immortal - out of the fire with the reflection that "Unknowing are ye mortals and thoughtless: ye know not whether good or evil approaches."

Demeter withdraws from the world her ripening powers and the earth becomes barren; all earthly prayers are then full of pleading for Demeter's anger to be assuaged. Finally Zeus reverses his original decision and sends word to Hades that Persephone should be returned to the upper world. Hades, while seeming to agree to this demand, tricks Persephone into eating a pomegranate seed (sometime said to be more than one) and thus he retains some power over her: for this reason she is said to rule with Hades in the underworld for four (or in some versions six) months of the year and during the remainder returns to her mother. As the Homeric hymn says:

"And all-seeing Zeus sent a messenger to them, rich-haired Rhea, to bring dark-cloaked Demeter to join the families of the gods: and he promised to give her what rights she should choose among the deathless gods and agreed that her daughter should go down for the third part of the circling year to darkness and gloom, but for the two parts should live with her mother and the other deathless gods. Thus he commands."

Hermes guided Persephone back from the dark world of the Host of Many, and Demeter was then said to give two gifts to mortals: the first, but lesser, was corn; the second, and greater, was the institution of the Eleusinian Mysteries.

That, then, is a brief outline of the myth of Persephone. There are some further mythological references to her which we will examine in the suggested interpretation.

Greek Names

Persephone: *bringer of death.*

Kore: *the virgin* - in fact she was always called this until Pamphos and then Homer named her Persephone.[2]

Demeter: form "De" a variation of Da, a very ancient Earth Goddess and "Meter" - *mother.*[3]

Okeanos: *Ocean*, the last of the seven Creative Gods, the 'separating intellect' who makes possible the distribution of intellectual souls each of which carries (latently) the intellectual paradigm of creation.

Eleusis: *the place of happy arrival*, related, according to Kerenyi to Elysion, that part of the underworld known as 'the isle of the blessed.'

Hecate: *Liddell & Scott* suggest the name derives from εκατος 'far-shooting' which was also a epithet of Apollo; it implies light penetrating darkness.

Hades: *Obscure* or *Dark*, suggests Plato in the *Cratylus.*

Nysa fields: from the same root as we derive Dionysus - an important point to which we will return in chapter four.

Demophoon: the *slayer of the people.*

Suggested Interpretation

Persephone has a curious place in mythology: from one point of view she is the innocent virgin who most represents the inexperienced soul at the outset of her journey. As a playmate of nymphs who are the daughters of Okeanos I think we must see her essential intellectual (or spiritual) nature implied. But the nymphs are, according to Porphyry,[4] that order of divine beings who supervise the *descent* of souls. This is because their affinity with moisture suggests a precipitation into matter; this is opposed to 'dry' souls, who, by their lightness, are ascending. Okeanos is the last of the seven Intellectual Deities of the Creative world: the seven Gods and Goddesses contemplate the eternal idea within the world immediately above their own - the archetypal world of the Intelligible-Intellectual Gods of Life. From this contemplation arises the manifested or 'projected' universe in which human souls are scattered like seeds in the dark earth. Okeanos' place in this scheme is to make the final separation of the complete intellectual or spiritual scheme into the myriad souls, each of which carries the whole creative idea in potentiality. His daughter-nymphs accompany the descending soul into the next level of reality (*i.e.* the order of soul, which is the first projection of intellect).

The flowers they are gathering are the childish objects in which Persephone and her friends see beauty. The narcissus flower is mentioned, and in some variations this is the very flower which opens up the earth to allow out the chariot of Hades. The myth of Narcissus, from which the flower gets its name, is a myth of the soul becoming enchanted by the *reflection of its own beauty* in matter.

Beauty and its reflection in matter are the allurements by
which Persephone is to step out of her enclosed childhood
and into the marriage with the 'Lord of Many', or Hades,
who rules over the dead. This is the first death the soul
suffers: the loss of the pure spiritual existence when she is
called to experience life in body.

Now as soon as the soul steps out of the purely spiritual
realm into the mundane sphere, she places herself in a
curious condition, which is not entirely spiritual, nor yet
entirely material: as a spiritual-corporeal being she at first
loses her full communion with pure spirit, without
immediately gaining a communion with the material realm.
For this reason the myth tells us that her shrill cry is heard
neither by immortal nor mortal. But now there is no
turning back, despite the loneliness: Persephone has
reached out with both hands, and is, therefore, committed
to the embrace of the wondrous flower. This, I think, is
the key to the true artist, who seeks to manifest the
infinite beauty of spirit in finite matter - stone, paint,
sound, words or whatever: it is, of course, an impossible
task, which drives many artists through agonies of
perceived failure.

Persephone's father, Zeus, lord of creation, has set a joy-
giving flower as an inevitable trap; for it is the will of the
Creator that his spirit will enter his creation in order to
give life to the otherwise inert matter. But the soul 'lives
the spirit's death and dies its life' - that is, by attaching
herself to matter, the soul must experience the cycle of life
and death so foreign to deathless spirit. Her sense of
spiritual unity is tested to the limit by the many-bloomed
plant, and is overwhelmed by the Host of Many.

From the point of view of mystical initiation this is the
first step, and one of aspiration and faith; for no new

initiate can know before this step is taken what really lies ahead on the mystical path. Most human beings have arrived at some kind of stasis in their relationship with the world which could, and often does for a while, pacify the deep-seated urge to rediscover their spiritual nature. To start out on the mystical path of initiation is to put at risk our mundane contentment for the sake of something unknown, and possibly frightening.

There is another aspect of Persephone: that of wife of Hades and Queen of the dead. In this aspect she is clearly not a virgin maid. Furthermore although she is described as dwelling in Hades in some seasons and in others with her mother above, this is, we must assume, a device to indicate her dual nature. There are several instances of mythological characters descending to the underworld to appeal to Persephone, *who is always there*: for example Orpheus turns to her when his unsuccessful petition for the return of Eurydike falls upon the cold ears of Hades. And again, Psyche's last task set by Aphrodite, in the myth of Cupid and Psyche, is to descend to the underworld to beg for one day's supply of Persephone's beauty for the Goddess.

What are we to make of Damascius' first line - '*The soul descends into generation, after the manner of Kore*'? Is he referring to the aspect of Persephone as maid, or that of wife and queen of Hades? Certainly, on the surface, it would seem that it is the former which fits the plan; but Kerenyi, in his book *Eleusis* looks long and hard at the implications of the bits of evidence still available to us regarding Demeter and Persephone. He comes to the conclusion that the two Goddesses are in some respects double, and merge into one another.[5] In an earlier part of the same work[6] there is an enquiry into the nature of the

blessings conferred on those who celebrated the mysteries
of Eleusis which is worth quoting here:

> But of the poets who speak of the Mysteries in the
> form of a beatitude, it is only Pindar who tells us
> something about their content. He speaks in such
> a way that the initiate could recognize the secret [of
> the Mysteries] in the words that cloaked it: "Blessed
> is he who, after beholding this, enters upon the way
> beneath the earth: he knows the end of life and its
> beginning given by Zeus!" 'End' and 'beginning'
> are seemingly colourless words. But they reminded
> the initiates of a vision in which the two were
> united.

Here, perhaps, is a clue to both the problem of mother and
daughter merging and the reason why Damascius begins
with Persephone and ends with Demeter - *for here the
beginning and the ending are, indeed, united.* Persephone as
Queen and Bride of Hades stands midway between
Persephone the maid, and Demeter the Mother: we cannot
entirely dismiss the second phase of Persephone in
considering the original descent of the soul, because it is
this very destiny which calls her to her adventure. It is
because her mother is queen of the living that Persephone
has the capacity to rule the dead.

To continue with our analysis of the myth story: The
nine days of searching without bathing or eating may well
tell us something about the preparations that the most
advanced initiates had to undergo before the final mystery
revelation of Eleusis. But it is also worth considering that
the number nine represents the abstraction of abstraction:
for nine is the product of three multiplied by three, and

three represents the abstract idea or form while four represents matter or manifestation.[†] Death 'abstracts' the soul from its manifesting body, so nine - or the intensified power of three - symbolises the reassertion of form over matter, or the enduring soul arising from the decaying body. The Romans, if at all possible, buried their dead on the ninth of the month and celebrated their memory in the ninth month (November) - as we still do on all-souls day, at the beginning of November - and especially commemorated their dead every ninth year. The fasting search, then, represents the need to purge the concerns of matter from our perception if we are to rediscover the soul lost in hyle (or matter). For while Persephone was, in her first aspect as virgin, ignorant of what may befall the spiritual being which is immersed in matter, Demeter was not: her meeting with Hecate, the ancient queen of night, represents the divine power to contemplate the material world without becoming involved in it. Hecate and Helios are good examples of what Joseph Campbell calls 'meetings with helpers' in the diagram of the previous chapter.

[†] See Taylor's *Theoretic Arithmetic of the Pythagoreans* for a fuller discussion of the inner qualities of number. Three is said to represent form or idea because three is the simplest number which allows thought - for each thing we think about must have, in some sense, a beginning, a middle and an end. Four introduces to the intelligible three an embodying fourth principle, and therefore allows manifestation: the minimum number of sides needed to produce a regular solid is four (the three sides, and base, of a triangular pyramid).

Do the four daughters of the royal house of Eleusis represent the uninitiated masses who do not recognise the presence of divinity even as she enters their home? Certainly the theme of ignorance is maintained throughout the episode with Demophoon.   There is a question regarding the whole episode of Demeter in disguise tending to Demophoon: why is she bothering with a stranger when her daughter is the object of her concern?   An early example of displacement activity?   The answer may, perhaps, be seen in the similarity of the name Persephone and Demophoon - 'bringer of death' and 'people slayer' respectively: does the myth tell us of their common identity? Is Demeter's plan to burn out the mortality of Demophoon really a plan to release the imprisoned soul of her daughter? We will return to consider the story of Demeter herself at a later point.

The remaining part of the myth (*i.e.* the story of Persephone's return) does not refer, I think, to the first stage of Campbell's hero-cycle, nor to Damascius' key to the Mysteries: the descent of the soul is in innocence. The rescue of the soul and her consequent upward path is the story of the following chapters.   It is worth pointing out that Campbell says that while it is possible to map out the various stages around the complete cycle of the hero soul, many myths related only a small arc of the circle, or at least concentrate on a part while implying the remainder. Persephone's guidance by Hermes, the quicksilver God of mind, from the realm of Hades, is the story of the experienced soul of later in the cycle, when she has learnt the means to cross the boundaries of life and death.

But the final symbol we must consider here is that of the pomegranate: the two most obvious features of the ripe fruit are the abundance of seeds and the blood colour and moisture of the juice. Here we may see that once the soul has started its descent it can easily fall further by taking to itself the stuff of generation: we will explore this in greater detail in the next chapter on Dionysus.

The first stage or initiation, then, is not primarily concerned with knowledge; rather, it is characterised by joy and openness. Kore stands as a pure intention which is untroubled by questions of self - indeed Persephone hardly knows herself and her eyes are full of the beauty which Zeus has set before her. Persephone's embrace of life and death requires a faith in the absolute goodness of the Gods, so that whatever state is entered upon is gladly accepted. The words of Socrates in the *Phædo*,[7] as he contemplates his imminent death, are worth recalling; after he has explained to his disciples that those that dwell in this realm are the subjects of beneficent rulers, the Gods, Cebes asks why Socrates does not fear a departure from this realm? His reply is as follows: "I shall depart to other Gods who are wise and good . . . . I shall go to Gods who are perfectly good rulers." From this foundation in faith the initiate may make the first steps towards *entelechy*, or the mystical goal of the soul, in happy aspiration. The goal may be seen as simply being a fully matured soul by which the breath of Zeus enters his creation and brings life to the dark deeps. To the Greeks the soul was known as *Psyche*, which means 'breath', while the Latin for soul is *anima*, or 'life.' It seems to me that animating the manifested cosmos is a noble and divine calling, and one that should never be forgotten in our struggles to rediscover our deepest spiritual nature. The many-bloomed flower that each of us plucks in our descent is so sweet, "that all wide heaven above and the whole earth and the sea's salt swell laughs for joy."

Notes

1. The details of the myth of Persephone are taken, except where indicated, from the Homeric *Hymn to Demeter* and the *Library* of Apollodorus.

2. *cf. Eleusis*, Kerenyi, p. 28.

3. *op. cit.* 2.

4. In his *Cave of the Nymphs* [TTS vol. II].

5. *op. cit.* 2, p. 148 ff.

6. *op. cit.* 2, p. 15.

7. *Phædo* 63b.

Chapter Four

Dionysus

She is scattered by generation, after the manner of Dionysus

The Myth[1]

The origins of Dionysus are, in keeping with his nature, confused; let us start with the best known story of his conception and birth.

Cadmus, king of Thebes, had four daughters: Semele, Ino, Agave and Autoneon. Of these four, the beauty of Semele attracted Zeus who lay with her and implanted his immortal seed in the mortal woman. But Hera, the first wife of the King of the Gods, was moved by jealousy and planned the destruction of her husband's lover, as well as the child which she carried within her womb: to this end she planted in Semele's mind a doubt as to the real identity of the father of her child. The only sure proof that he was indeed Zeus, was, Hera suggested, that he should appear in his true form, rather than the disguise of mortality which Zeus had put on to lie with Semele. Thus it was that the princess asked of Zeus a favour, to which he agreed; she then demanded that he appear before her unveiled by illusion. Unable to refuse what he had promised, he was forced to comply, and stood before Semele in the full heat and force of his lightning and thundrous essence: as no mortal can withstand such untempered power, she was

immediately destroyed. But Zeus took the unborn child
from her disintegrating body while cooling tendrils of ivy
protected it from the intense heat of the Father, who,
taking the role of mother, sewed him into his thigh.

So it was that Dionysus was born a second time, from
the miraculous womb of his Father, but still Hera's
jealousy pursued the child, who was being cared for by
nymphs: some sources say these nymphs became afraid and
others that they were driven insane, and so he was given
into the keeping of his aunt, Ino, who brought him up in
a grotto. In an attempt to keep him from the destructive
power of Hera, Ino dressed him as a girl and later, Zeus
disguised him as a goat. Hera, however, inspired the
Titans, the gigantic divine offspring of an earlier generation
of Gods, to capture the boy Dionysus, in this episode
known as Zagreus.

This particular myth is the central one as far as
Damascius was concerned. According to Westerink's notes
on the *Commentary on the Phædo*,[2] the episode begins with
Zeus placing Dionysus on his Throne and announcing that
his son was to rule the world. Hera's jealousy being thus
inflamed, she incites the Titans to destroy the God.
Apollo, standing beside the throne delivered a warning
about the plot, but to no avail. The Titans ensnared
Dionysus by disguising themselves as Bacchae (followers of
Dionysus), and presenting him with games and playthings -
for he was but a child: the toy which finally trapped the
divine child was a mirror. Once captured the pretend
Bacchae gave him not a sceptre - as befits the ruler of the

world - but a thyrsus made of a fennel stalk. The monstrous giants then tore him to pieces and prepared to devour him; his torn members were first boiled in water and then roasted over a fire. But while they feasted on the cooked flesh, Zeus, excited by the rising steam, and perceiving the cruel act, hurled his thunderbolt at the Titans. There followed a battle between the titanic giants and the Gods, during which the uneaten heart of Zagreus was gathered up by Athene; the Titans were defeated and from their burning ashes mankind was generated.

Afterwards, Zeus commanded Apollo, Dionysus' half-brother, to bury the scattered limbs of the slain youth according to custom, and this being done, Dionysus was regenerated from the preserved heart by Athene; having been restored to pristine life and vigour, he took his place among the Olympic Gods - the only one born of a mortal woman.

This, in outline, is the myth of Dionysus' many births. There are, however, many mythological adventures related of this God, for example:

Dionysus wandered the earth bringing to man the knowledge of the vine, as well as the mystic orgies which were forever after associated with him. Homer tells of Dionysus, together with his nurses and followers, being attacked by Lykourgos, king of Thrace. His nymphs were dealt savage blows in this attack and Dionysus himself was forced to flee into the sea where he was received and protected by Thetis. For the outrage of attacking a God, Lykourgos was first blinded and then killed (there are several variations on this death, including one in which he dies because he cut off his own foot, mistaking it for a vine). There are several similar episodes in which male opposition to Dionysus but female support end in disaster for those who resist the God; the theme of dismemberment is often repeated (see also Euripides' *Bacchae*). The fable of Orpheus and Eurydike ends with the female celebrants of Dionysus tearing Orpheus apart.

In his journeyings (according to the Homeric hymns) Dionysus was captured by pirates who believed he would fetch a good ransom: the helmsman immediately perceived that they had made prisoner of a God, but the other sailors persisted in their folly. However once the pirate ship was under sail, Dionysus' bonds fell away and the mast of the ship began to grow vine and ivy tendrils. Wine, too, began to flow through the ship and the God himself was transformed into a roaring beast; the pirates, all except the helmsman, threw themselves into the sea and were changed into dolphins.

Dionysus was married to Ariadne who, being a mortal, was given the gift of immortality by Zeus, according to Hesiod's *Theogony*. Curiously there are tales of Ariadne's death: confusion of death and life once again playing its full part with all things concerned with Dionysus. In the *Nekuia*, Odysseus sees her in the Underworld and notes that she was killed by Artemis on the island of Naxos (or Iraklion, Crete). Here the fate of Ariadne is intertwined with the myth of Theseus and the Minotaur: it is Ariadne, the half-sister of the monster of the labyrinth, who supplies

Theseus with the golden thread which allowed him to descend into the underground prison-maze without becoming lost in it. Once Theseus has killed the Minotaur he takes Ariadne to Dia (Naxos) where, according to one version, Athene appears to Theseus in a dream and commands him to abandon Ariadne there. Dionysus then seduces her with a crown of gold.

Other strands of the myth of Dionysus have him descending to the underworld to raise his mother, Semele, to the upper world where she becomes an immortal of Olympus. After this she is known as Thyone - 'bride of God.'

Dionysus has several names - Bakcheios, Iakchos, Theoinos, and Bromios, for example. He was celebrated by torch-lit processions throughout ancient Greece, and his symbols, apart from the vine and ivy already mentioned, include wild cats (especially the panther) and the thyrsus of the fennel stalk. He was the presiding deity of Grecian Thebes, and the tales of Sophocles concerning Oedipus, king of Thebes, and his daughter Antigone are well worth considering in the light of the characteristics of the God.

Following on from our consideration of Persephone, the Queen of the underworld, we must not be surprised to find that Dionysus is intimately concerned with this dark region. Indeed, Heraclitus says,[3] "for if it were not Dionysus for whom they held their processions and sang their songs, it would be a completely shameful act to the reverent; Hades and Dionysus, for whom they go mad and rage, *are one and the same*." Orpheus says of him that he was "Of Zeus and Persephone, occultly born", while he is also said to "sleep in the house of Persephone." Time and again the myths of this God offer to us opposites: death and life, gentleness and violence, pleasure and pain. A common depiction of his female followers in Greek art was as suckling wild animals - and thus the most gentle of human activities was married to the ferocity of nature. Duality, it seems, is his essence.

In the sacred precincts of Delphi, Dionysus was said to preside for the (winter) third of the year in which his half-brother, Apollo, departed - again an echo of a motif found in the myth of Persephone.

Greek Names

Dionysus: The *Dio* beginning to this name is from the genitive of Zeus, but the remainder is less clear - it could be a reference to Nysos, a locality, so that the name means 'of Zeus born in Nysos'; but it also may be a Thracian variation of the Greek word for son, in which case the name may mean 'son of God'

Semele is the Phrygian name for the Goddess of Earth.

Titan: based on the root which means 'particular' or 'certain', the Titans are the Divinities of the world of the 'separated particular' - the material world. They are the artificers of the ultimate manifestation at the base, as it were, of the pyramid of the universe.

Bromios, means 'strong'.

Suggested Interpretation

The words of Damascius, that "the soul is scattered by
generation, in the manner of Dionysus," are clearly
indicated whatever aspect of this myth we consider. To be
scattered one must be broken up: separation, therefore, is
of the essence of the Dionysian story. Almost from
conception Dionysus brings in his train death and
destruction, madness and deception, overwhelming life and
death.

Semele, whether one accepts her as a representative of the
mortal condition, or whether one sees her as an expression
of the great Earth Goddess, in her coupling with Zeus, the
great 'sky God' of the Greek Pantheon, is doomed to
disintegration, for the power of the spirit always breaks
open the enclosed body. Her later resurrection indicates,
perhaps, that the death of the natural body may be the
discovery of the immortality of the hidden inner self.
Zeus is the God who produces the projected universe by
the power of his 'at oneness' with the subjective archetype
of the universe: he is supplier of spiritual power to passive
matter, which is the key to understanding what in human
terms we would describe as his promiscuous behaviour - he
seeks to impregnate all the objective world with his
immortal spirit.

Soul, as soul, is the lowest principle which is whole in
itself, and self-contained; when living in conjunction with
pure intellect this whole is without parts; when the soul
acts within herself she is a whole made up of parts; with
the descent into generation, the soul, in some respect,

sacrifices this self-contained wholeness and must separate her parts into discrete units. Each of these parts is dependent on something outside itself, and life for the soul in generation is like ivy, which always depends upon some greater life for its support. Likewise the soul is said, at this point, to be under the rulership of the moon, whose different phases display a partitiveness and a dependence upon time. The growth of ivy is governed by the moon.

Dionysus is not born once, but must suffer three births: the first from the ruined womb of Semele, the second from the thigh of Zeus, and the third from the heart saved by Athene, the Virgin Goddess of Wisdom. Birth represents a source, a starting point of life: a triple birth, therefore, indicates a multiple nature, rather than a simple oneness. Persephone is torn away from her mother, which represents a division of sorts: but Dionysus is torn away first from his mother, then from his father, and finally from himself - the ultimate division.

Hera, who rules the procession which is begun by the creative power of Zeus, is very often the apparent opposition which turns the potential hero into an actual hero: "This," says Aeschylus, "Zeus ever decrees, that wisdom is not attained except through suffering." Hera is the Goddess who stimulates the seed of Zeus so that the inherent divinity will be brought into manifestation. But as the Demiurgic Gods rule the limit of the eternal realm, all that is projected from them is, in some way, subject to the change and opposition which characterises that which is below the eternal world. Thus Dionysus is the God who so often appears in disguises, and the male god whose

first period is spent dressed as a girl: for while the eternal
is what it is, the projected world often appears to be what
it is not. Dionysus' disguise as goat takes this motif even
further, for now he does not even appear to be the same
species as his real self: further, the goat is representative of
the appetitive aspect of nature, being famed for its
voracious eating and for its sexual powers. Gods whose
kingdoms are natural are often portrayed as horned: Pan,
Dionysus and Persephone, according to Porphyry's treatise
On Cult Images,[4] were so portrayed, with goat-like horns.
The same author gives a wonderful display of myth
interpretation in his treatise *On the Cave of the Nymphs*;
here he shows[5] how the characteristics of a cave are
symbolical of the material world - we need look no further
for the meaning of Dionysus' sojourn in his childhood
cave. (Plato, of course, too, uses the cave as a
representation of the world of sense in the *Republic*.[6])
With his ever-changing childhood, full of disguises and full
of guardians unable to remain stable in his presence,
Dionysus arrives at his defining moment allured by an
image of himself in a mirror: here we see the theme of
separation replayed - for now he contemplates himself and
an image of himself as separated out. In this state he falls
into the power of the Titans, whose rulership is of the
zoned world of matter, where each thing is distinct from
every other thing. It is interesting to note that part of the
Titans' plot involved them disguising themselves as Bacchae
and the substitution of the regal sceptre with a fennel stalk:
the deception of matter, which by taking on various forms
appears to be something other than it really is, is thus

symbolised - and indicates how the soul, given a potential rulership over her own mundane universe, is often misled by her inability to distinguish the real from the unreal, when she first comes into contact with the material realms. The thyrsus is a particularly appropriate substitute, for it is a stalk of knots and separate chambers - thus signifying rulership over the world of zones and particularities. Dionysus has been called the monad of the Titans - that is to say, he is their unifying and causal pattern: as such, the Titans appearing as Bacchae is not inappropriate, although their attack on him reverses the proper order of monad to multiplicity. (One is reminded of the fairy story *The Goose Girl*, in which a princess suffers when a maid-servant usurps her place during a journey to be married in a distant kingdom.) The unsuspecting child is torn apart and his separated members disintegrated by water and fire, the two great destructive forces of nature. But from the cooking flesh of his son, Zeus is alerted by the steam which ascends to the sky to his peril: thus we see that even in the lowest depths, a subtle essence of the soul seeks always to rise to its king and father, and that the providential communion of soul with her maker is never broken.

We must pause here in our overview of the myth of Dionysus, since this is the crucial point to which the commentary of Damascius leads. Up to this moment we can see the soul descending through the higher worlds, called by her destiny, Dionysus-Hades. But the scattering into generation is effected by the allurement of her own image in the reflection of the mundane world: like

Narcissus she is plunged into the waters of death, loving the appearance of a most beautiful being, which, in truth, is her own form.

The magic of a mirror is brought to our attention in myth, fairy story, and folk tale, time and time again. The mirror in these stories often shows the protagonist a new world, or a vision of a different reality, which makes an insistent demand on the seer: what the soul must do is to use the vision to discover the truth, and to make the new world her own. The problem faced here is one of identification: the image is not the reality; the face in the mirror is not the self, *but* it is the means whereby a partial intellect (that is to say an intellectual being who has not fully unfolded her intellectual nature) finds reality, and comes to know herself. The reflective capacity of intellect allows the soul to consider the most abstract ideas, which are properly resident only in the eternal world, as well as the sensible world in terms of reasons. "Look not upon Nature," says the Chaldæan Oracle, "for her name is fatal."[7] The reflective faculty allows us to look not directly at Nature, but upon her image, and, just as Perseus was enabled to accomplish his task of severing the head of the Gorgon with the polished shield of Athene acting as the intermediary between him and the petrifying Gorgon, so the soul may arrange nature without losing herself, by using this faculty. It is the path of the soul to seek the beauty which the mirror reminds us is waiting to be found. The danger is not the reflection, but our misunderstanding of the reflection - the attributing to the image a reality greater than it deserves - and it is for this reason that the Oracle warns of its fatal name (or power).

The mystic who seeks complete initiation must pass this way: the faith we must carry within us as we take the initiation of Persephone, blooms into the love of Dionysus which is based on the faith that our heart is immortal and will regenerate by the power of the saviours Apollo and Athene.

The fight of the Olympian Gods against the Titans represents the apparent contradictions which arise when the 'convertive' and 'spiritward' tending impulses ruled by the Olympic Gods mix with the downward and material tendencies ruled by the Titanic Gods. For Dionysus, touching the lowest extremity of the Natural order (and full of its energies), is the monad of the material order; the divine powers are then extended into the lowest and most-remote-from-The-One reaches of the universe, by the characteristic activity arranged by the Titans. But the Olympic Gods are those Gods which spiritualise the mundane world, and collect all things back into The One: we will see in later chapters how this is accomplished especially through the wisdom of Athene, and by the unitive power of Apollon. In this myth these two divinities are central to the return and final rebirth on Olympia of Dionysus.

Among the so-called intellectual community of the modern world there has been a movement to view ancient myth as an allegory for the natural world and no more. The regeneration of Dionysus from his heart can, quite obviously, be construed as merely a symbol of the power of a seed to regenerate a new plant during the winter months, as can the myths of Osiris, Christ, John Barleycorn, and many others. Dionysus, as first recipient of the Natural Order, is quite rightly called a Vegetative Deity: but we must be very clear here: *the natural world is as it is because of the characteristics of the Gods - not vice-versa.* Dionysus sets the pattern whereby the cycles of nature may preserve life amidst the changing circumstances of time, place and condition. All things for which he is responsible will follow his paradigm, and that is why Orpheus, an arch-priest of this God, was said to have been torn apart by frenzied women after his return from Hades, and afterwards became an oracle of truth on the island of Lesbos.

To generalise somewhat concerning human society, it is the male who tends to try to control nature, and to impose on civilisation a clear boundary of 'moral' behaviour. The whole thrust of technological society is the impulse to control nature, and to control the natural side of our own natures. The female, conversely, tends to co-operation rather than control, and immersion in nature rather than 'riding upon it' or conquest. Dionysus, being the ruler of generation, in which boundaries are continually crossed, and in which experience is mixed with knowledge, is on the side of women, and women are on his side. The boundaries, whether they are between life and death, between male and female, between the human world and the natural world, spirit and matter, dreaming and waking, or whatever, are the points of danger as well as the points of opportunity for growth. (Botanists will confirm that

growth invariably takes place at the extremity of plants -
the border between the plants' being and non-being.)
Dionysus' mystic orgies and rulership of wine both
challenge the established order of things: those who hold
mundane power are rarely happy at the advent of the
celebrations of this God, and often repress - or attempt to
repress - him and his impulses. Euripides' play *The Bacchæ*,
has a scene in which Pentheus, king of Thebes, tries to
stamp out the worship of Dionysus which has been
introduced into his kingdom: to do so he captures the God
(who is, typically, in disguise as one of his own priests) and
puts him into the dark dungeon in his palace. Alas! within
a short space of time the chains which bind Dionysus are
broken (in fact he had never been bound, because in reality
his place had been taken by a bull), and a fire breaks out.
The tragic king - whose destiny is to be torn apart by the
wild women worshippers of the God - led by his own
mother, now rushes here and there hurling and tilting at
phantom images of Dionysus, and fighting the fire. No
finer image of the dangers of repressing the natural
instincts and powers of nature, instead of giving them
proper exercise, has been staged, to my knowledge.

The pirate episode, too, is an interesting one from the
point of view of the power of Dionysus to overwhelm
those who at one and the same time bind him and draw
him closer to themselves. Suddenly the artificial vessel, so
much under control, and so much the master of the waters
upon which it sails, becomes a thing of living nature, with
roaring beasts and the blood-red wine let loose. The
pirates, recently the arrogant masters of the sea are driven

into its waves, changing form and losing their humanity. Only the helmsman who had recognised the God survived.

Ariadne, Dionysus' wife - who is immortal but also seen in Hades - has herself connections with many mythological characters. Above all she is sister of the half-man, half-bull monster of the labyrinth and the one who supplies the golden thread by which Theseus is enabled to descend into the darkness of the killing maze, slay the minotaur, and find his way back out. A woman, then, who lives close to the borderland of nature and man, and of life and death, immortality and mortality, monstrosity and normality.

In the diagram already given from Campbell's *Hero with a Thousand Faces* (p. 36) we see Dionysus ruling the descending horizon, while his half-brother, Apollo, rules the ascending horizon: in Delphi these two are joined in a single sanctuary. We will see in a later chapter how characteristic it is for Apollo firstly to seek to prevent the separation of Dionysus (by standing near his throne and warning him of the threat of the Titans) and, once the separation has taken place, to seek to bring things back into unity.

The word 'tragedy' comes from the root in Greek which means 'goat' and refers to the rulership of drama by Dionysus, who is often depicted in the guise of a goat: in the myth we saw that he was protected from the wrath of Hera by being transformed into a goat. Aristotle defines the purpose of tragic drama as that of providing for its participants (performers and audience) a catharsis: in Dionysus, we find the God who will, indeed, cathartically purge the soul of its complacency, assumptions and illusions. With Dionysus we are plunged into an alien environment: Plato, in the *Phædo*,[8] says, that the soul is drawn by the body "to things which never subsist according to the same, [she] wanders and is agitated, and becomes *giddy like one intoxicated*" as she contacts that which is so foreign to her spiritual and stable essence - Plato, therefore, very clearly suggests that the newly embodied soul is in the power of Dionysus, the God of wine. A vase painting of Dionysus now in the British Museum shows the God clearly staggering under the influence of wine (see plate 2). The effect of wine, of course, is to depress those areas of the brain by which the mind connects, controls and unifies diverse experiences and thoughts: thus the drinker speaks truth normally suppressed for the sake of social obligation, and performs acts normally inhibited by social norms. Is this a good or bad thing? The ambiguity with which we may view such a state is echoed by the epithets attributed to Dionysus: "the delight of mortals", the "god of many joys", the "bestower of riches", the "benefactor", the "eater of raw flesh", the "render of men" and he who "delights in the sword and bloodshed", to mention a few.

In the Persephone initiation we are required to ask "what is my destiny?" but in the initiation of Dionysus we are required to ask the more fundamental question "what am I?" For the shallow knowledge of the self which has sufficed until this moment is exposed for the first time as a ridiculous shadow: the inherent questioning nature of the soul arises and we are embarrassed by our own ignorance.

Notes

1. The myths of Dionysus are drawn largely from the Homeric *Hymns to Dionysus* (numbers 1, 7 and 2); the Orphic *Hymn to Dionysus* (including Damascius' exposition of the Orphic tale, in his *Commentary on the Phædo*, during the section in which the seven myth verse is presented - I, 131); and Euripides' *Bacchae*.

2. *Commentary on the Phædo*, Westerink, North Holland Press, 1976, vol. II, p. 26.

3. Fragment 15 (Diels).

4. Porphyry *On Cult Images*, fr. 9, trans. E H Gifford.

5. Porphyry *On the Cave of the Nymphs* p. 147 - 148 of TTS vol. II.

6. See the beginning of book seven of the *Republic*.

7. TTS vol. VII, p. 37. The word *fatal* is, of course, being used in its most exact sense, signifying that a thing is bound up with the workings of the Fates. Anything which is fatal is subject to the measurements involved with time, and therefore participates in the infinite and eternal energies of Providence only indirectly.

8. *Phædo* 79c.

Chapter Five

Prometheus

Like Prometheus and the Titans, she is bound to body.

The Myth[1]

Prometheus is a second generation Titan and related, therefore, to the antagonists of Dionysus (see previous chapter). He is the son of the Titans - Iapetos and Klymene - although in some tellings he is the son of Gaia with either an unnamed father or none at all; in the Titanomachæ or 'war of the giants' Prometheus sided with the Olympian Gods and, as a result, was not hurled into Tartarus, as were most of the defeated Titans. It is reported that Prometheus made a decisive contribution to the Olympian cause with his advice to Zeus that he should secure his thunderbolts and release the Cyclops.

In Hesiod's *Works and Days*[2] there is an account of the five ages of mankind: each age gives way to its successor, in a descending scale. Of the first two ages, those of Gold and of Silver, the intervention of Prometheus is not required, but at some point in man's descent Prometheus becomes their champion. There is even a myth[3] which says that it was Prometheus who fashioned man from clay, and that Zeus then breathed spirit into the inert body to give him life. But the central myth is that Prometheus realised that man was in a vulnerable and wretched condition and resolved to bring to his aid the heavenly fire of Zeus. Plato says[4] that his brother Epimetheus had given all the gifts of nature - strength, speed, claws, wings, and so on - to the various creatures of the earth, but had forgotten man, and had, therefore, left man without any natural protection. Prometheus' plan to bring fire to man was, however, contrary to the will of Zeus; the Titan was obliged, therefore, to steal the fire concealed in a fennel stalk.

With fire, humanity was able to rise above the other creatures of nature, and the whole earth was enkindled with the light of the divine fire: when this came to the notice of Zeus he was enraged, contending that with fire man would threaten heaven itself. The father of Gods and men decreed that Prometheus should be punished, and that man, too, should be weakened so that his threat to the Gods would be diminished.

The Olympian Gods created a woman to bring ruin to mankind, with each God endowing her with a gift which would serve as a lure to Epimetheus - who was to be the bridge between mortals and the immortals - taking the woman as his wife and fathering the present race of men.

Hephaistos mixed earth and water, and from this clay made a woman in the image of the Goddesses, endowed with both voice and strength; Athene taught her weaving; Aphrodite poured *charis* and the inciting of desire about her; Hermes gave to her a scheming and thievish character, as well as lies and a flattering tongue; Athene dressed her with the help of the Charites and Peitho, who put golden chains around her; and the Horai gave her a crown of spring flowers; she was also given a wondrous crown by Athene which had been made by Hephaistos, upon which were fashioned all kinds of monsters. The woman was named Pandora, because she was a gift to man from all the Gods. With Pandora came a jar with a lid, which was not to be opened. Hesiod seems to suggest that Pandora understood in advance what the consequences of opening the jar would be, but she still removed the lid - and thus unleashed from its dark receptacle all the ills which now torment the world. Only one evil was left trapped in the jar, *elpis*, or 'expectation' - and thus the despair which might have overwhelmed mankind once the other evils had been released was avoided.

Zeus then turned his attention to the punishment of Prometheus. His crime of the theft of fire was, it seems, not his first offence against Zeus: some time before, Prometheus had arranged the first sacrifice of the flesh of cattle to the father of the Gods, but had wrapped the best of the meat in the intestines, and, conversely, disguised the white bones in a layer of succulent fat. He had thus tricked Zeus into choosing the worst of the carcass, preserving the best for man, and setting a precedent which was forever after followed as the prototypal pattern for sacrifice. Hesiod says that it was because of his anger at this deception that Zeus had withheld his fire from the race of men.

The punishment of Prometheus that Zeus decreed was that the Titan should be taken to the Caucasian mountains by Kratos and Bia and chained to a rock (or possibly impaled upon a column); further, that an eagle (or vulture) should eat the immortal liver of Prometheus by day, the organ regenerating itself every night (see plate 3). In some versions the bird feasts on the liver every other day, the intermediate day allowing for the regrowth. This punishment was originally set to be perpetual.

So Prometheus remained until eventually Heracles came upon him during his series of twelve labours; there is some confusion as to whether Heracles then acted on his own initiative or whether he had been commanded by Zeus to free the firestealer. Some versions of the myth suggest that there was a deal struck between Zeus and Prometheus - the Titan gaining his freedom in return for revealing prophetic knowledge concerning Zeus. It seems, in this version, that Prometheus knew which Goddess would bear Zeus a son who would overthrow him, and that just before Zeus coupled with Thetis, he warned the king of the Gods that it was this Goddess who was to be avoided. Heracles shot the tormenting bird with an arrow and then broke the chains which held Prometheus to the cold mountains of the Caucasians.

But whereas the agent of Prometheus' release is Heracles, it is Hermes who is the go-between: it is he who tells the chained Titan "Do not expect any end to this suffering before someone of the Gods presents himself to be a recipient of your pain, and volunteers to go down into sunless Hades and the murky depths of Tartarus." This is sometimes taken as a reference to the centaur Cheiron, but may be a reference to Heracles who is to become a God and whose labours do indeed take him voluntarily into Hades. It is Prometheus, by the way, who helps the hero perform his most mystical labour: the gaining of the golden apples of the Hesperides. Prometheus advises Heracles to approach Atlas, himself a surviving brother Titan, and offer to take the Giant's place in holding up the sky if Atlas will go and win the golden apples.

An important festival in Athens arose from the cult of Prometheus in which youths raced through the city carrying torches. Athens was the only site, as far as we know, that had an altar and cult of Prometheus: the practice of torch races was copied from this original festival so that the celebrations of Athene and Pan and others included similar races. Plato's *Republic* opens with reference to the festival of Bendidian - dedicated to Artemis - and another torch race.

Greek Names

Prometheus, lit. 'before thought: most take this to mean the thought that comes before experience or the rational *a priori* knowledge which is, at best, prophetic; but it could be taken to mean that deep knowledge which is of the intelligible-intellectual order - the order prior to the intellectual order.

Epimetheus, lit. 'after thought': which in contradistinction to the above is that knowledge which is gained from experience, or the *a posteriori* knowledge which is the province of doxastic (or opinion-based) man. Again, in line with the second interpretation of Prometheus, it could be taken to mean that knowledge which is of the natural order, which is below both the intellectual and the psychical orders.

Titan - see previous chapter's 'Greek Names'.

Zeus: 'God' (the Z is properly pronounced as an 'sd' so that one can easily see the connection with the word Deus.)

Pandora from *pan* - all, and *dora* - gift. The normal interpretation is that the name denotes someone who was all-gifted, but strictly speaking it should be taken as referring to the fact that she was produced and arrayed by *all* the gods as a gift to Epimetheus.

Kratos, 'power'.

Bia, 'life'.

Heracles - 'the glory of Hera'.

Suggested interpretation

After the soul has crossed over the threshold into the material realms, under the auspices of Dionysus, she must next undergo a series of trials in order to make sense of the world in which she finds herself: in this she imitates Prometheus.

The story of Prometheus has some difficult narrative episodes for the myth-makers who unfolded it, largely caused by the fact that both Zeus and Prometheus are prophetic and yet must act as if they were not. Furthermore, each God seems not to know things which the other does; this must be interpreted as a difference in intellectual centre. Prometheus, we must suppose, knew the consequences of stealing the fire of Zeus - the torment of being chained and eaten alive upon the Caucasian mountains - and yet still chose his destined course. The soul, too, according to Plato in the tenth book of the *Republic*,[†] knows the course of her terrestrial life before descending. In the myth of Er, she has examined her chosen life before crossing the arid plain and drinking the waters of Lethe; these waters of forgetfulness are primarily provided so that the memory of her heavenly station is not

[†] The myth of Er is covered in the tenth book, sections 614 to 621; at 619c Er tells of a rash soul who chose a life, but did so without care so that, having made the choice and *then* examining the details of the life, "he wailed and lamented his choice, not having observed the admonitions of the prophet" (who had counselled prudence to all those souls choosing their lives at that point).

a distraction as the soul turns her attention to the material world. The myth of Prometheus is the story, then, of a voluntary acceptance of a limitation foreign to the real nature of the protagonist. Once chosen, of course, the limitation appears to be involuntary, as both Prometheus in our story and the soul in reality must wait on events which unfold in time.

The Titans are the offspring of a pre-Olympian generation of Gods and Goddesses; they tell us something about the relationship of Intelligible Gods to the Gods of Matter. In the scheme of the six choirs of Gods, and the worlds which spring from them, the intellect is reflected in soul; life is reflected in nature; and being is reflected in matter (see figures 5a & 5b). Thus the primordial Gods, who may be considered as more powerful than the Olympian Gods, give rise to the Titans who are defeated by Zeus and his brethren. The word 'titan' is derived from the Greek root τι 'ti' which means *particular*; they are the divinities who rule the furthest reaches of the universe - the order of ultimate separation and particularisation. This order is the most distant from the order of being, in which all things are gathered into one, for the whole universe is, as Thomas Taylor puts it, 'connectedly contained' in being's occult causality; however it is the closest order to being from the point of view of its essential component - pure matter - which has the effects of all the other orders occultly impressed upon it, and yet in some manner retains the characteristic of a simple uniformity.

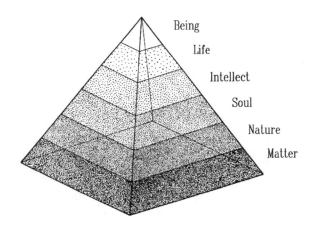

Being
Life
Intellect
Soul
Nature
Matter

Figure 5a (above) showing the "pyramid of being" divided into the six orders or worlds. **Figure 5b** (below) showing the relation of the three higher worlds to the three lower, if the lower worlds are seen as a reflection of the higher. At the apex of the pyramid is the super-essential One, to which the "convertive" or "returning" Mundane Gods move things; at the base is non-being to which the disintegrative and particularising Titans move things.

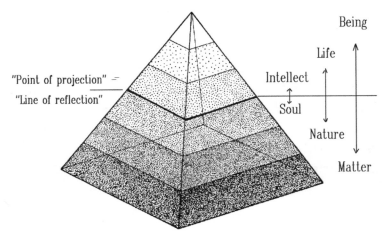

"Point of projection" =
"Line of reflection"

Being
Life
Intellect
Soul
Nature
Matter

The Titanomachæ, or war of the giants, represents the apparent conflict between the movement ruled by the Titans of increasing separation and flight from The One, and the movement ruled by the Olympian Gods which is convertive, or a return of all manifested things to The One. The mundane order is not quite the material order: the latter is the order of receptivity while the former is the order in which the arranging energies of the soul, the vivifying energies of nature, and the receptive capacities of matter are conjoined. In the mundane world, therefore, there is a continual tendency to build more and more sophisticated bodies and kingdoms: from the pre-elemental matter of stars arises the elements; from the elements arises the compounds of the mineral kingdom; from the mineral kingdom arises the vegetable kingdom; from the vegetable kingdom arises the animal kingdom; at the height of the animal kingdom arises the subtleties which allow the human soul to form its own kingdom. But for all this to unfold, the mundane Gods must ensure that the disintegrative and passive tendencies of matter are limited and held in the lowest position. Thus the battle between the Titans and the brethren of Zeus is a necessary preliminary to the production of the mundane realm; and the hurling of the Titans into Tartarus, the lowest level of Hades, represents the proper ordering of the passivity of matter within the whole scheme.

There is a common misconception that Hades is the Greek form of what we know as hell. In fact Hades is both paradise and hell; it is the realm in which the effects of 'good' and 'bad' actions are finally received. Within

Hades there are the blessed isles of the Elysian fields as well as the place of punishment, which is called Tartarus. Tartarus is, however, only a punishment because it is the place of extreme division and separation, a state which is most alien to the soul (which is the manifesting expression of the One). In Tartarus, souls which have lived a disintegrative terrestrial life undergo the purgation which must follow such a life: *it is not punishment for the sake of punishment, but a purgation for the sake of the recovery of the soul's essential purity.* But even in this lowest of all realms it is the will of the perfect One that there is a rulership of Gods, for thus the providential energies of divinity are extended to the furthest reaches of the universe. The Titans are the Gods to whom this rulership is given.

Why then are there said to be Titans left above Tartarus after their defeat? Deep within the body there is a wisdom which reflects the primordial thought of the intelligible realm; this profundity is not rejected by Zeus but embraced and utilised for the benefit of the perfection of the projected universe. Thus Atlas is given the duty of holding apart the sky from the earth - a duty which is only accomplished by the greatest strength, but one which is still separative. (We have, by the way, already come across a Titan, Okeanos, who is said to be of the Intellectual choir of Gods - his is the lowest rulership of the Intellectual or Creative order, in which the intellective reasons are *separated* before they are passed on into souls.) The brothers Epimetheus and Prometheus become the means by which the two tendencies of the human mortal - the proceeding and the convertive - are governed within the proper limits of manifestation. Prometheus advises Zeus on the deployment of primitive forces, the Cyclops and the thunderbolts, for it is he, as a Titan, who knows when such things can be safely utilised. Now, as we have seen before, it is the destiny of the soul, when she has philosophised properly to "nearly govern and arrange the universe in conjunction with Zeus" as Maximus Tyrius wrote: we govern by imitating the Father of all, and we too must, therefore, embrace the profundities of the Titans. One cannot over-emphasize the need to embrace the foundations of the mundane realm rather than reject them; the need to distance oneself from materia, as taught by Plato and his followers (as well as other religious and philosophical leaders), should not be misinterpreted as a rejection of materia. The mystic's initiation into the mysteries of Prometheus is the *voluntary acceptance* of the limitations of matter, not its *rejection*.

What are we to understand by Hesiod's five ages of man - those of gold, silver, bronze, heroic and iron? Perhaps we should consider whether it is possible for the soul to descend from its pristine state of pure spirit to the terrestrial realms with no intermediate steps. Plato taught that it was not possible for the pure to touch the impure, nor for like to touch unlike. It is an essential element of the beauty of the universal scheme that all things are unfolded in an orderly manner, and that there should be no empty gaps between principles and their manifestation. Thus the orderly unfoldment of the soul - a principle in the proper sense of the word - towards its ultimate expression is in gradual stages. This can be understood both in terms of time, and in terms of simultaneously experienced 'lives.' In the golden age the soul is purely spiritual, and lives in communion with the Gods (soul as soul); in the silver age the soul lives as a thinking entity in communion with reasons (soul as mind); in the bronze age the soul lives as a feeling entity in communion with emotions (soul as heart); in the heroic age, the soul lives as a willing, or volitional, entity in communion with purposes (soul as will); and in the iron age soul lives as an embodied entity in communion with the most outward universe (soul in body). At the highest level, that of gold, life is without trial because in the spiritual realms things *are* immediately they are willed, without process: but as each descending level is lived, so trials are more and more clearly experienced, for process becomes increasingly dominant at each succeeding level. One might consider each lower level as a separation from the principle at the heart of the previous one: the silver age, for example, is a separation from pure spirit. When man has separated from the light of pure mind he requires some divine champion to bring the fire back into his sphere. It is for this reason that Prometheus became so important to the lower races of humanity.

But the fire of creative intellect sits in lower worlds only with difficulty and with a degree of danger to its inhabitants. The symbolism of the rising flame reminds us that fire always seeks to return to the heavens. The fire which was constrained in the hollow of a fennel stalk is not easily retained upon the earth, and thus the theft is said to be against the will of Zeus. The contradiction of spirit trapped in objectivity is the central problem of the myth of Prometheus: that which is without process cannot be entirely contained in that which is within process. The evils that have befallen the human race are, in truth, the misuse of man's higher faculties in the lower realms; he does, indeed, threaten heaven in the sense that he can pervert the unfoldment of the good in the objective realms.

There are two ways in which the power of spirit can be safely exercised in the projected universe of materiality: firstly through the lessons gained by experience, and secondly through the raising of the finite consciousness to the realm of the infinite. The providential care of the Gods extends to the soul the opportunity to learn through experience by the means of Pandora and her jar of apparent evils: in the same way that receptive matter 'seeks' to experience form, so the myth maker uses the symbolism of the receptive aspect of the feminine as that which seeks experience. To many this is a frightening departure from the status quo, and several cultures have grown up with a fear of the female aspect of the soul, with all the potential for suffering that experience brings. Eve (from the hebrew meaning *life*) and Pandora are burdened with the blame which those who fear the departure into manifestation find easiest to externalise upon woman. But Pandora, in truth, represents the wisdom which the ever-giving Gods bestow upon mundane souls through the instrument of suffering. Epimetheus is the divine power that rules the soul who is, for the present, operating mainly below the level of abstract reason. The gifts which the Gods give Pandora are the traps of appearance: it is in the process of discovering the reality behind the appearance that the soul exercises her latent powers of reason.

The second salvation of the soul who is to wield spiritual power in the material world, is the upliftment of consciousness to the level of abstract reason. Upon this path it is Prometheus who is the inspective guardian of the soul. It is Prometheus who teaches mankind the higher arts, the deeper wisdom, the divine sciences; his governances are treated as perpetual paradigms for the soul acting in the mundane world. Let us take the example of the first sacrifice to the Gods: Hesiod relates that when this was made, Prometheus in his cunning disguised the bones under a layer of succulent fat, and, conversely, disguised the best flesh under a layer of intestine, and then invited Zeus to chose the first share, as befits a God. The portion left would be that which man would be allowed to eat after the sacrifice. Now the narrative becomes difficult here, because Hesiod does not want to portray Zeus as being unable to see through the trick; nevertheless, the Father of Gods and men, almighty Zeus, chooses the bony portion and from that time on in the ancient Greek world when sacrifices were made, it was the Gods who were given the inedible parts, the best flesh being distributed to the participating mortals as a holy feast. No doubt there are several interpretations one can put forward concerning this division of meat: perhaps it is appropriate that the ever-living Gods should receive the most enduring part of the animal - the bones - while mortals, whose time is fleeting, should receive the most transient part of the body. The important point, however, is the fact that Prometheus' division was the pattern which men accepted as the guiding model for all their theurgic actions. If, as some authors report, the withholding of the fire from man by Zeus was because of this trick, we may say that in choosing the transient flesh (with was covered by the least attractive part of the body), man is choosing the material life, and is, therefore, self-exiled from the realm of fire.

Prometheus sees effects within causes; Epimetheus sees effects only when they have unfolded. In the myth Prometheus warns his brother about accepting the gift of Pandora from the Gods, and then, once accepted, about leaving the woman in charge of her jar. Epimetheus is the one who squanders the natural talents among the animals of nature, leaving men bereft of the means of surviving in the world; Prometheus is the one who sees and foresees the misery this state of affairs will offer man, and who, therefore, sets about rectifying the situation. As we have said, Prometheus is the inspective guardian of the rational soul: but we need to be clear that his is the descending arc of the cycle of the soul. It is only the lower race of humanity, having departed from the purely spiritual life, who have need of his providence; his actions may not be directed to such a low level as those of Epimetheus, but they are certainly concerned with the soul who is involved in process and generation. Because this sphere is a real limitation of what is properly free, the voluntary sacrifice is necessary. Prometheus is bound to the rock, just as Christ is nailed to the cross and Osiris is locked into the coffin-trap designed by *his* brother.

Aeschylus names the servants of Zeus who bind Prometheus as Kratos (power) and Bia (life): thus we see that it is the extension of spirit into the realm of manifested power and life which is the crucial factor in the soul's tormenting confinement in matter. Prescient or not, there is always, it seems, a chaining of the soul in the downward movement of the journey: Pandora was given golden chains as an adornment, while Prometheus is given chains as a punishment - both bind the soul to the lower realm.   There is, perhaps, a difference between these chains: the chains which adorn Pandora are renewed every time the soul chooses the sense life and, therefore, the chains are never thrown off while we live the terrestrial life; the chains of Prometheus, which seem to be of a perpetual nature are, in truth, of a finite duration. Prometheus must wait patiently, remaining true to his prophetic vision, knowing that the inherent spiritual truth that he holds within will eventually be the means by which he is reconciled to Zeus. Likewise the soul, if she remains centred in her spiritual self, even while manifesting in the realms of matter, will be released from her limitations.

The imprisonment of Prometheus is made all the more tortuous by the activity of the eagle (or vulture) which is set to feed on his liver.   This is symbolical of the characteristic duality of the realms of generation with its continual growth and decay, its alternating life and death, which is so foreign to the spiritual being. To the Greeks the liver was the seat of the lower desires, which, says Plato, are characterised by the search for increase and decrease, the indrawing and expelling of things into and from the body, and which is never at rest.[5] To modern science the liver is the organ of discrimination, since it is the organ which purifies the blood of poisons: this by no means runs counter to the myth of Prometheus who, from one point of view, represents the soul who is learning to discriminate the real from the unreal through her involvement in matter.

The full involvement of Heracles in the freeing of Prometheus will be discussed in the following chapter, but a few observations on this episode directly concerning the plight of Prometheus will suffice the present chapter. Prometheus has waited patiently for his release, knowing (as he is prophetic in nature) that the hero will, in his labours, break the chains which bind the Titan. Prometheus' task is not to break the binding himself, but to retain his deep knowledge of the *moira* or fate of the Gods. His advice to Heracles concerning the performance of the labour to obtain the golden apples of the Hesperides is of a similar characteristic: that Heracles should not himself go to the garden of the Hesperides, to the extreme west of the world, but should arrange that Atlas, a Titan, should take his place in the quest, while Heracles temporarily takes on the task of Atlas in holding the sky away from the earth. The golden apples, according to Sallust,[6] represent the whole mundane world (it was the rolling of a golden apple into the feast of the Gods which caused discord to arise and the dispute between three Goddesses as to who was the most beautiful: the judgement of Paris, in favour of Aphrodite, resulted in the Trojan war). In the final embrace of the mundane world by the soul, it is wise to use the intermediary of a divinity who is concerned with the particular, and thus the soul retains an immunity from the attachments which may arise from too close an involvement with particulars.

One final point which might be worth considering here is the horizontal alignment between the various Divinities of this cycle. We have already given Campbell's diagram which shows the axis between the crossing and the recrossing of the threshold - in other words the axis of Dionysus-Apollo; but we can see that there are, in fact, three pairings Persephone-Demeter, Dionysus-Apollo, and Prometheus-Athena.   These three pairings can be diagrammatically represented so (figure 6):

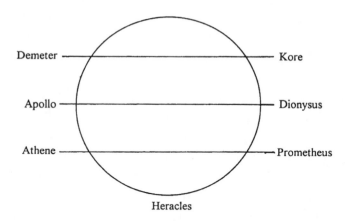

Figure 6 The three pairs of mythological figures.

Ancient Athens, the city of Athene, was, according to modern scholarship, the only known site of a cult temple to Prometheus. The torch races, so common in the festivals of Athene's city, were, it is thought, based on an original which was the celebration of Prometheus, the fire-bringer.[7] Athene and Prometheus are the most notable assistants in Zeus' war against the Titans; both, in their own way, are the Divinities who excel in the power to awaken wisdom within the human soul.

We have seen that the initiation of Persephone requires the question "what is my destiny?" and that the initiation of Dionysus requires the question "what am I?"; I suggest that the initiation of Prometheus requires the soul to ask "what am I not?" For here the limitations and contradictions which are a necessary consequence of an essentially spiritual being falling into materiality become the predominating concern. We will see in the next chapter how it is the role of the true hero to overcome limitations - but the awareness of such limitations is, of course, an essential preliminary to their eventual conquest. It is through definition (literally to bring limit to terms and concepts) that we are able to start to explore truth: the initiation of Prometheus is, therefore, the initiation into truth.

Notes

1.   The details of the myth of Prometheus are drawn largely from Hesiod, who relates some aspects of the myth in his *Theogony* and others in *Works and Days*, and from Aeschylus, who wrote three plays concerning the myth, of which only one is extant; these are *Prometheus Pyrphoros* ('Firekindler'), *Prometheus Demotes* ('Bound') and *Prometheus Lyomenos* ('Unbound') - only fragments and comments of later authors and philosophers remain of *Firekindler* and *Unbound*.

2.   *Works and Days*, 110 ff.

3.   Apollodorus, I, 7, 1.

4.   See the *Protagoras* 320d - 322d.

5.   *cf.* Plato's *Timæus* 71a - b, and his *Gorgias* 493e.

6.   Sallust *On the Gods and the World*, ch. 4. [TTS vol. IV]

7.   See page 47 of H W Parke's *The Festivals of the Athenians*, Thames and Hudson.

Chapter Six

Heracles

She frees herself by exercising the Strength of Heracles

The Myth[1]

The stories concerning Heracles (or Hercules) are, I think, the most numerous in the surviving Ancient Greek myth corpus, and for the sake of clarity in this one chapter, I have summarised and abridged the myths fairly ruthlessly.

Heracles was the son of Zeus by Alkmene, who was married to Amphitryon; ancient sources suggest that Zeus seduced Alkmene in some disguise, possibly the form of Amphitryon himself, while her husband was in exile or fighting abroad.

Again Hera's jealousy is aroused by the liaison and its offspring: as a result, she sends a serpent to the nursery of the baby Heracles, who strangles it with his bare hands. Thus begins the life of Greece's most loved hero.

Like most Greek mythological heroes, however, there are ambiguities of character about Heracles, which give pause for thought: we will see later on that he murdered both his own wife and his children. Another story about his earliest years concerns a trick of Hermes (or in some versions Athene) who takes the young child to Hera and persuades the Goddess to feed the child - whose identity she does not know - from her own breast. Either because she discovers his identity, or because the feeding Heracles sucks too hard, she then pushes him away, and her milk spills, forming, as a result, the milky way; the pseudo Eratosthenes informs us that it had been ordained that no son of Zeus might obtain heavenly honours unless he had fed at the breast of Hera.

Heracles had several teachers during his childhood, including Linos who, when teaching him music, struck his pupil who, being enraged, returned the blow and killed the teacher. Another teacher was Cheiron, a Centaur, whom he was later to wound accidentally with an arrow poisoned with the blood of the Hydra which Heracles had slain: Cheiron, to escape the torment of the poison, voluntarily entered Hades, even though he was an immortal. (See the previous chapter.)

On reaching early manhood, Heracles performed various deeds which marked him out as a hero: he was said to have killed a lion (at Kithairon) which had been destroying livestock around the kingdom of Thespios. Thespios had forty-nine (or, in some versions, fifty) daughters: Heracles had intercourse with all of them - in one night according to Pausanias, in seven nights according to Herodoros or in fifty nights if we are to follow the writings of Apollodoros. It is Pausanias who makes the number of girls forty-nine, the fiftieth refusing Heracles and, as a result, being made a priestess with perpetual virginity; after which, as Gantz points out, the lion seems rather a simple matter. Heracles wrestled with Death in order to recover Alkestis who had volunteered to take her husband's place in Death's kingdom. Another deed is leadership of the Thebans in their victory over the Orchomenians who had collected tribute from Thebes for many years as a punishment for past wrongs. (A similar episode occurs in Virgil's *Æneaed*.)

In the *Nekuia²* it is reported that Megara, daughter of Kreon, was married to Heracles, and two later authors suggest that this was a reward for help which the hero had rendered the Thebans. Some authors report that Hera sent Iris and Lyssa (madness) to Heracles, who in a fit of insanity killed his wife and children, the latter (who number anything between 2 and 8) by throwing them on a fire. Some other versions merely say that strangers killed his family. Euripides has Heracles nearly murdering his step-father, Amphitryon - a deed only avoided by Athene throwing a stone at the hero's head to knock him unconscious. There is an appealing balance in Heracles' death, which was the result of the jealousy of Deianeira (his second wife): she spread the poison from the Hydra - which had already caused Cheiron's descent into Hades - on the inside of a chiton, or robe, with which Heracles was accustomed to dress when sacrificing to Zeus (see plate 5). The poison, becoming activated by the heat of the sacrificial flames, caused the chiton to cling to Heracles' skin and burn like acid; he commands a helper to build a funeral pyre, planning that death will relieve him of his suffering. But Zeus elevates Heracles to Olympus and confers on him immortality - as well as release from his pain. Most artistic depictions of Heracles' ascent to Olympus show him being led into the company of the Gods by Athene.

An element of the Heracles myth which should be
pointed out is the regularity with which our hero wounds
or threatens to wound the Gods and Goddesses: in the
various storylines, he is said by some authors to have
wounded Hera, Ares, and Hades as well as having
threatened Helios and Okeanos, and having been the cause
of Cheiron descending to the realm of Hades. Heracles is
the slayer of second and third generation Titans, and of
others who have a qualified immortality. There is a story,
too, that Heracles attempted to steal the tripod which was
the oracular seat of the priestess at Delphi so that he could
establish his own oracle; Apollo, to whom the priestess and
the oracular sanctuary were dedicated, intervened to
prevent the theft and the two fought over the tripod: Zeus
hurled a thunderbolt to break up the fight. The scene is
depicted on the surviving stone decorations at Delphi.

For this last transgression (or, alternatively, because
Heracles broke the laws of hospitality and murdered a host
and his sons in a dispute over the host's daughter) he was
sold into slavery for three years during which time he was
obliged to perform various tasks. According to some
writers these were of the usual heroic kind - conquering
cities, and so on - but according to others Heracles was
obliged to wear women's clothing, spin and card wool, and
was beaten with a slipper. Yet others record that he was
set to work in a vineyard, where he caused havoc.

Heracles is in some way associated with the best known
of Greek exploits or at least episodes which suggest them,
even when he has no great part to play: he was an
argonaut with Jason; he sacks Troy in revenge for wrongs

the Trojans commit; like Odysseus he was subjected to a storm on leaving Troy and is separated from his companions; his battle against a giant, on the exact spot upon which the Olympian Gods fought the Titans, is an echo of this earlier conflict.

The Twelve Labours

From the above brief details, one can see that the myths of Heracles are very extensive, and that he performed many tasks. However, he is perhaps best known for a series of deeds known as the 'Labours of Heracles,' which we will now consider. These Labours were not always identified as a particular series, but were written about in various collections from very early sources: when the Temple of Zeus used twelve episodes from the life of Heracles as decorations for its metopes, they became, so to speak, a canon. Because of their somewhat piecemeal beginnings, the order in which they were performed is subject to many variations. I will deal with them in conformity with the writings of Diodoros (which are very nearly the same as Apollodoros'), and recommend Timothy Gantz's *Early Greek Myths* to the student who is interested in the different sequences given to them by ancient authors and artists.

Introduction

All twelve labours in this series were set for Heracles by his cousin, Eurystheus, king of Mycenæ. The reason why

Heracles obeys his cousin and undertakes the tasks is
somewhat difficult to clarify: some versions have it that
Heracles wished to return with his family from exile to the
kingdom and therefore promised Eurystheus that he would
tame the earth; others that the labours were undertaken as
expiation for his murders; others that he was instructed to
accomplish the labours by the Oracle at Delphi as a means
to achieve apotheosis (Campbell's fourth stage - see page
37). It was also said that when Alkmene was pregnant
with Heracles, Zeus announced that the child born on the
day upon which he was due would have dominion over
other men. Hera, however, contrived to delay the birth of
Heracles and hastened the birth of a cousin, Eurystheus, so
that the announcement worked against Zeus' son who was
obliged to do as Eurystheus ordered by the command of
his own father.

I - The Nemean Lion

The first labour is that of the Nemean Lion, a monstrous
creature with an invulnerable hide, which had been
ravaging the country around Mycenæ. Heracles was the
guest of Molochos before starting out on the labour which
had been set, like the other twelve, by Eurystheus;
Heracles told Molochos to offer a sacrifice to Zeus if he
was successful, but to himself as a hero if he had not
returned within 30 days.

The lion was the offspring of Chimaira and Orthos, part
of the early divine generation of primitive forces originally
descended from Gaia and Pontos (Earth and Ocean), and

said to have been raised by Hera. Heracles at first attacks it, without success, with weapons - arrows, sword, and club - but its protective hide forces him to change his tactics, and so eventually he drives it into a cave with two entrances, one of which he blocks up, and there strangles it with his bare hands. He returns to the house of Molochos on the thirtieth day, and from there makes his way back to Eurystheus, who, being terrified at the sight of the Lion, even though it was dead, commands that henceforth Heracles should wait outside the city gates at the end of his expeditions.

Heracles, not one to miss the opportunity to gain advantage from his exploits, determines to make the invulnerable hide into a protective cloak for himself, and, finding that no instrument could penetrate the skin, he uses the lion's own claws to scrape and shape it. Ancient depictions of Heracles usually show him in this distinctive cloak.

II - *The Hydra of Lerna*

The Hydra was the offspring of Echidna and Typhoeus (part of the Pontos-Gaia family) and, therefore, closely related to the Nemian Lion; according to some, the Hydra was the grandmother of the Lion. This monster had many heads, which had the property of regenerating if they were cut off - two, in fact, growing in the place of an original - and one head which was immortal. It lived by a spring in the swamp of Lerna, feeding its huge body by making raids on the cattle of the surrounding countryside.

Heracles, on the advice of Athene, attacks the Hydra with normal weapons and uses fire to cauterise each neck before a head could regrow. During this attack Heracles is distracted by a giant crab which, on the prompting of Hera, crawls from the sea and nips him. (Some writers report that because of this he was assisted by his companion Iolaos and others that Iolaos was involved in the whole attack anyway.) Eventually Heracles manages to decapitate the immortal head and buries it beneath a rock. A final act in this episode is the gathering of the blood of the Hydra for use as poison on Heracles' arrows, again the hero seeking gain from his labours, but one for which, as we have seen, Heracles paid dearly.

III - The Erymanthian Boar

Eurystheus next commands Heracles to deal with an enormous and savage boar which had devastated the forest of Erymantheus in Arcadia; further, he orders, Heracles must bring back the beast alive. This labour is accomplished by the tactic of driving the boar into deep snow, and thus trapped it is captured in a net by the hero who lifts it on to his shoulders and takes it back to the king. Eurystheus is so frightened by the savage appearance of the boar that he jumps into a *pithos*, or large jar, in order to hide from it and his captor. It is during his return with the boar, says Apollonios, that word came to Heracles of the quest of the Golden Fleece upon which he would accompany Jason. Further, it is said to be while Heracles was journeying to the Forest of Erymantheus that he became involved in the fight with Centaurs in which he accidentally wounds Cheiron, his former teacher. The fight arises because his host, a Centaur named Pholos, opens a jar of wine, the fumes of which attract other Centaurs who begin to quarrel over it; Heracles defends his host and routs his attackers who flee to the dwelling of Cheiron, and it is here that his arrow accidentally wounds the teacher in the knee. The wound proves incurable and the only escape for the agonized Centaur is to exchange his immortality for someone's mortality. Some speculate that this is the cause of his descent into Hades in order to fulfil the prophecy concerning the release of Prometheus, but it is more likely that the exchange of immortality and mortality is with Heracles himself, and thus the freeing of Prometheus is inextricably linked to the apotheosis of Heracles.

IV · *The Keryneian Hind*

The next labour is the capture, alive, of the golden horned Hind of Mount Keryneia, sacred to Artemis. Kallimachos says that the hind was one of five which drew the virgin Goddess' chariot, and that it had escaped at the behest of Hera, especially to provide another task for Heracles.

Our hero pursues the swift Hind from her home in Arcadia to the region of the Hyperboreans and then back to its starting point, the entire chase taking one year. At this point Heracles' patience seems to be exhausted and he wounds it with an arrow; in many versions Artemis and her brother Apollo appear at this point to preserve the life of the Hind, which Heracles then carries back to Eurystheus.

V · *The Stymphalian Birds*

There is a lake in Arcadia, deep in a black forest, called Stymphalis which had become infested with a great number of ferocious birds, possibly originating from an island in the Black Sea sacred to Ares, but driven to Stymphalis through fear of wolves: Eurystheus commands Heracles to rid the forest of these birds, which according to some versions had feathers which could be fired like arrows, and to others, were man-eating. To accomplish this task Heracles uses a bronze rattle - made by Hephaistos, and given to the hero by Athene - which scatters the birds into the air; once airborne he shoots some of them with arrows, while others return to their island. On the metope on the Temple of Zeus at Olympia the labour is represented by a scene in which Heracles hands a number of birds to Athene.

VI · *The Stables of Augeias*

Eurystheus orders Heracles to clean the stables of Augeias, king of Elis, whose stables of 3,000 oxen had not been cleaned for 30 years; this task, said Eurystheus, was to be completed in one day. This seemingly impossible labour is successfully accomplished when the hero diverts two rivers, the Alpheus and Peneus, through the stables.

Once done, Heracles demands payment from Augeias of one-tenth of the oxen (according to some this had been agreed beforehand) but Augeias argues that the labour was the command of Eurystheus and therefore no payment should be made. The dispute, although it seems Heracles was not paid, caused considerable ill-consequences for Augeias.

VII - The Cretan Bull

Eurystheus now bids Heracles capture the Cretan Bull. The exact origin of this bull is confused: some writers report that it was the bull which carried Europa across the sea to Crete (not in these versions Zeus himself in disguise), but others that it was the one presented to King Minos by Poseidon, who had heard the king's prayer that he might have a bull worthy as a sacrifice to Zeus. In this last version the pure white bull, which arose from Poseidon's kingdom of the sea, became too great a temptation for Minos who, rather than sacrifice it to the Gods, put it with his herd of cattle for breeding purposes. This was to have disastrous consequences, for his wife, Pasiphæ, was sent a madness from the Gods in which she became enamoured of the bull: she mated with the animal and was delivered of the half-man, half-bull Minotaur to whom the youths and maidens of Athens were sacrificed until Theseus performed his heroics in the Minotaur's labyrinth.

Heracles travels to Crete and, with the permission of Minos, captures the bull which since the failure of the king to sacrifice it had become wild; he then rides across the sea back to the Peloponessos. The bull is set free on the Greek mainland, and is later captured and sacrificed to Apollo by Theseus.

VIII - *The Mares of Diomedes*

The next labour undertaken is the taming of the four man-eating Mares of Diomedes, king of Kikones and son of Ares. Heracles captures the Mares and leads them away, giving them to the keeping of his ally Abderos, while he returns with a band of men to fight Diomedes and his Thracian warriors: although Heracles succeeds and defeats the king, the four Mares meanwhile have torn apart Abderos. Heracles feeds Diomedes to the horses - for it was this king who had initially taught them their dire eating habits - and this action returns them to their natural inoffensive state. The animals are taken to Eurystheus who releases them, and they are eventually killed by wild animals on Mount Olympus. It was during this labour that Heracles was guest of Admentos and wrestled with Death in order to save his host's wife, Alkestis, from a premature descent into Hades.

IX - *The Belt of Hippolyte*

Eurystheus then commands Heracles to obtain the *zoster* (a war belt, worn outside armour) that Ares gave to Hippolyte, queen of the Amazons. The king, perhaps, intended to give his daughter, Admete (a priestess[3] of Hera), the belt as a gift.

Heracles requests Hippolyte to yield to him the zoster, and this is well received by the queen; however Hera stirs up the other Amazons, with the rumour that Hippolyte herself is to be carried off, and Heracles is attacked. Believing the attack belies treachery, the hero kills the Amazon queen, and takes the belt. There are other versions, in which the belt is given without bloodshed, and one in which Heracles gains his object by ambushing Melanippe, Hippolyte's sister, who is then ransomed for the belt. In many representations of this labour, Heracles is accompanied by several Greek heroes.

X - *The Cattle of Geryoneus*

Heracles is next ordered to capture the Red Cattle of Geryoneus, the three-headed (or three-bodied) and winged son of Chysoar and Kallirhoe (descended from the Pontos-Gaia line, already discussed in the First Labour); this order initiates a complex quest.

Heracles' journey to Erytheia, the dwelling-place of Geryoneus, is from East to West, and at some point on this journey he threatens Helios, God of the Sun, with his arrows: for this audacity Helios lends him the golden barque upon which the Sun sails the ocean in his night journey from his setting place in the West to his rising place at the Gates of Dawn. Okeanos sends a storm to rock the barque, but Heracles threatens him too, and so completes his voyage, at the end of which he sets up the

Pillars of Heracles at the mouth of the Mediterranean sea. Upon setting foot on Erytheia he is attacked by the herdsman of Geryoneus, one Eurytion, but Heracles kills him and his two-headed dog, Orthos. As the cattle are driven off, triple-formed Geryoneus himself attacks the hero, in an attempt to prevent the theft: he, too, is killed. The start of the journey back, with the cattle, is in the golden barque, but Heracles returns this to Helios and makes the greater part of the return by foot. This return is marked by a series of attempted thefts: in France the first attempt is made to steal the cattle by Ialebion and Derkymos (sons of Poseidon); in Italy it is Cacus who next tries - and nearly succeeds - by the subterfuge of driving the cattle away backwards while Heracles is asleep until the trick is given away by one of the cattle lowing; in Sicily Eryx is the would-be thief. All his foes are killed, and Heracles then makes his way back to Eurystheus. Different authors give conflicting versions to this last stage of the journey from Sicily onwards: one has Hera sending a gadfly to stampede the cattle, with Heracles only managing to calm them when they have reached northern Thrace; another has a snakewoman, perhaps Echidna, stealing Heracles' chariot's horses in Scythia; another has Neleus (and sons) attempting to steal the cattle in Messenia. Nevertheless the hero eventually wins through and hands the cattle over to Eurystheus, who in some versions sacrifices them to Hera. There is a tradition that Heracles set up colonies and cult centres on his long homeward journey.

XI · *Keberos*

This labour, too, takes place to the west, which was traditionally the way to the kingdom of Hades, guarded by a many-headed dog, Keberos: Eurystheus bids Heracles bring up from the underworld this mighty dog.

Heracles first presents himself for ritual purification and then full initiation into the Eleusinian mysteries (plate 4). Thus prepared, he descends into the kingdom of Hades with Hermes, and possibly Athene: in some versions his descent is easy and even the taking of the dog is facilitated by Persephone; in other version Heracles must wrestle with various inhabitants of the dark regions and negotiate with Hades for his dog. There is a suggestion that Heracles can take the dog if he does not use force, or at least iron; there are many depictions of this labour, and Heracles is usually shown overpowering the dog with his bare hands, or with a club, or even enticing it as one would a pet dog.

During his journey in the underworld he sacrifices one of Hades' cows (Odysseus makes a similar sacrifice in his descent into the underworld); he also frees Theseus from that kingdom, and lifts the stone which has been placed on Askalaphos by Demeter as a punishment for his revelation that Persephone ate seeds from the pomegranate.

The hero takes Keberos to Eurystheus, who again takes refuge in his pithos. The dog is then returned to its rightful place, at the entrance of Hades, where he continues to ensure those from the upper realm do not enter Hades before their time, and those from Hades do not return along the path of Avernus.

XII · The Apples of the Hesperides

When Hera married Zeus the Great Earth Mother, Gaia, gave to the queen a wedding present of Golden Apples growing on a tree, which was placed in the Garden of the Hesperides for safe keeping, and, to guard against the Hesperides themselves eating the apples, a giant snake was placed at the base of the tree. Eurystheus commanded his cousin to bring him three of the Golden Apples.

Heracles journeys through North Africa - from west to east - and is challenged to single combat by Cycnos, son of Ares, whom he kills: Ares then threatens the hero and would have tried to revenge his son's death, had not Zeus hurled a thunderbolt to separate the two. Later on his journey in this area he confronts three opponents - Anataios, Bousiris and Emathion - whom he kills. He then learns from Nereus (after catching him while asleep and wrestling with him) where the apples are to be found and from Prometheus how they are to be acquired: the Titan's advice is that Heracles should not himself attempt to harvest the apples, but should leave this to Atlas, a brother Titan. After freeing Prometheus from his punishment, Heracles travels to Atlas and agrees to hold up the sky - Atlas' task set by Zeus, from the time of the defeat of the Titans - while he goes to the garden of the Hesperides. The Hesperides are, in fact, the daughters of Atlas, so presumably this is the reason why he is able to fulfil the quest. On returning to Heracles, Atlas announces that he will take the apples to Eurystheus himself: the cunning hero, however, asks Atlas to hold the sky while he arranges a cushion between his shoulders and the sky before continuing, and once the Titan is back in place Heracles takes the apples and departs.

The apples, once shown to Eurystheus, are given to Hera who asks Athene to take them back to be replaced upon the tree.

There is another version of the labour, in which Heracles himself goes to the garden and wrestles with the snake before obtaining the apples. The garden is usually set in the far west, but again there is an alternative which sets it in the north, among the Hyperboreans.

Greek Names

Heracles, the 'glory of Hera' because it is the opposition of Hera that draws out the inherent greatness of Heracles.

Eurystheus, eury = broad, theus = god; signifying the manifestation of god, which urges Heracles to unfold his strength. The anonymous writer of the *Shrine of Wisdom* magazine article[4] on the Labours of Heracles suggests he is symbolical of the inner monitor of the soul - the guiding dæmon which urges the soul to fulfil its destiny.

Alkmene, bodily strength.

Deianeira, perhaps means 'terrible virgin.'

Hero, according to Plato (*Cratylus*, 398d) is based on the word 'love' - Ερος - because a hero arises from the love of a God for a mortal maid, or from the love of a Goddess for a mortal man. A hero, then, is soul as most clearly full of divinity.

Other meanings connected with the twelve labours will be dealt with as each labour is discussed.

Suggested interpretation of the general myth

There are many heroes of ancient Greek mythology, but none so revered as Heracles, and none with so great a body of stories or artistic representation. Heracles represents the ultimate manifestation of the human potential as lord of the mundane realm. With Heracles our circle has moved as far from the starting point as it is destined to do: he represents the turning point from which a translation back into the realms of spirit begins. It is for this reason, perhaps, that Heracles' relations with Gods, women and children are so ambiguous.

Heracles had a epithet as 'woman-hater' and his madness in which he slaughtered his first wife and children must be seen, I think, as a means for conveying the fact that, from one point of view, the return to the spiritual realm is a turning away from generation. Of course, from another point of view, Heracles was immensely fertile, as befits a man renowned for his impact upon the world. His intercourse with Thespios' forty-nine daughters, though, perhaps indicates that his fertility was centred not in his bodily strength, but in his relation to Zeus and the spiritual intellect of his father: for Zeus is said to be a seven-fold creator and forty-nine is seven to the squared power. We are reminded that the Chaldean Oracles advise[5] the soul not to deepen the square into the cubed power, and Heracles is the model of the wise-counselled soul. The throwing of his children back into the fire - a symbol of their grandfather, Zeus - indicates the direction in which Heracles' powers are turning. His killing of his teachers,

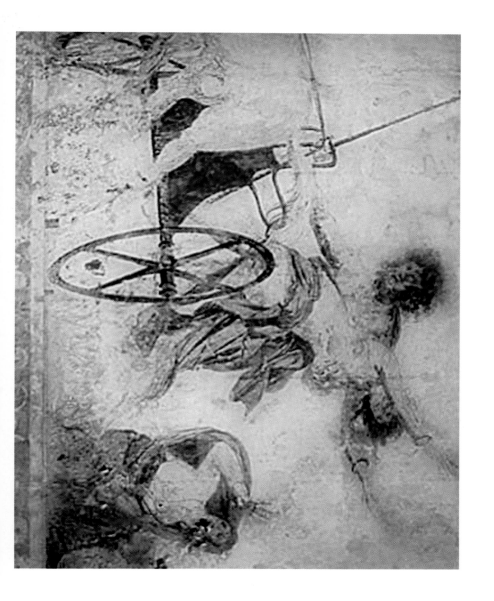

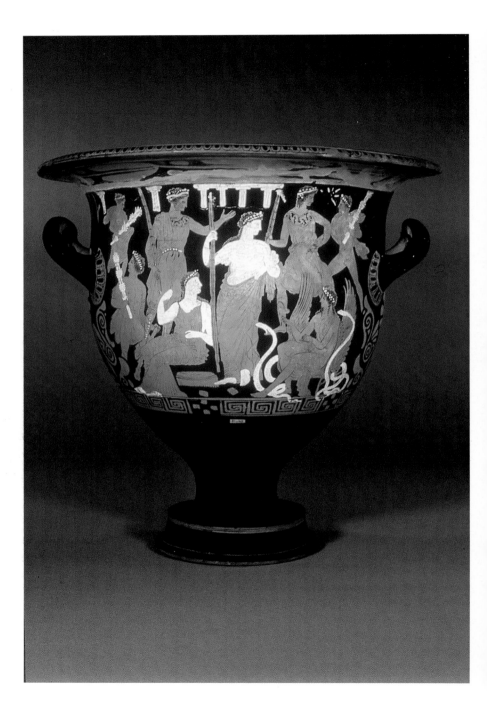

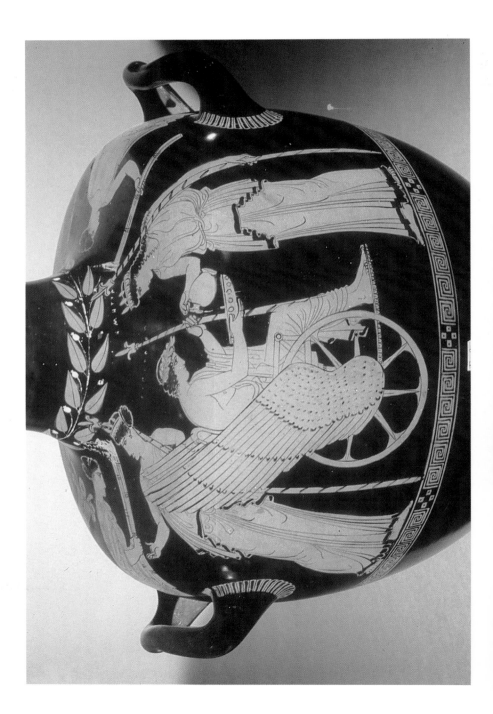

too, is a similar symbol, for the teacher 'leads out' the soul (thus the word 'educate') and this leading out, again, must stop at the turning point of the circle.

It might also be added here that Heracles as 'woman-hater' and, if you like, as the most masculine of the seven mythological figures in Damascius' cycle, is the furthest removed from the essence of spiritual soul, who is traditionally referred to as 'she.' It is, I think, another indication that Heracles as mundane hero has had to explore the furthest limits of spirituality in materia - a denial of self to find self.

As regards Heracles' relations with the Gods, it too is no more than one would expect at the extremity of the circle of the soul's journey. In the fullest mundane manifestation of its divine powers, the soul may be said to have constrained and limited the infinite: in this paradox is centred the wonderful ambiguity of the Greek hero. The story of Heracles' servitude, in which the great man was obliged to live as a slave and as a woman, once again shows us the inherent contradictions of a spiritual being - which is what the soul truly is - held in a material world.

The appearance - or where he does not appear, the echo of an appearance - in virtually all the great episodes of Greek mythology, is an indication of the comprehensive activity of the soul, once it has developed its faculties. Heracles' death again brings to the forefront of the myth his relation to the fire, which his father has planted within him. His end is signalled by the acid-like burning of his cloak - a symbol itself of the body which enwraps the soul - which becomes unbearable to the hero. He therefore causes a fire to be kindled, in order that his mortal part can be sacrificed, to the liberation of his immortal essence. The name of his wife who gives him this cloak, Deianeira, which means terrible virgin, fore-shadows our next mythological phase - that of Athene, the warlike virgin Goddess, who urges the hero from the sphere of action towards the divine world of Olympus.

The whole of the Heracles myth is one of overcoming the limitations which had become so apparent in the Prometheus stage of soul's initiation. If the latter's question during initiation is "what am I not?" (or, in other words, "what are my limitations?") this initiation prompts the soul to ask, "what powers do I possess for the assimilation of that which is 'not I'?"

Suggested interpretation of the Twelve Labours

The strength of Heracles, of which Damascius wrote, is his virtue - perhaps better understood if we start from the equivalent Greek word αρετη *arete*, which indicates a strength or an intensification. From the root of this word, αρι, we also find Ares, as well as the word for an oaktree, αρια. *Arete* indicates the power each thing has to express its own essential nature and, thereby, to reach its proper end, or *entelechy* - which is the goodness or excellence of a thing. We must return again to the curious position which the lowest extremity of the circle holds: it is the point at which the soul is most human, and yet it is also the point at which it starts the return path by which the human discovers divinity within.

What are the virtues which are symbolised by the labours of Heracles? They are undoubtedly those virtues which are properly human, or, in other words, those virtues which are exercised by the rational soul in its capacity as an animating principle in the mundane realm. Before we identify these virtues we need a brief survey of the entire range of virtues, and to this end I will turn to Thomas Taylor's notes on Plato's *Phædo*:[6]

> The first of the virtues are the physical, which are common to brutes, being mingled with the temperaments, and for the most part contrary to each other; or rather pertaining to the animal. . . The ethical virtues, which are above these, are ingenerated by custom and a certain right opinion, and are the virtues of children when well educated. These virtues also are to be found in some brute animals. They likewise transcend the temperaments, and on this account are not contrary to each other. . . . In the third rank above these are the political virtues, which pertain to reason alone; for they are scientific. But they are the virtues of reason adorning the irrational part[†] as its instrument; through prudence adorning the gnostic, through fortitude the irascible, and through temperance the desiderative power; but adorning all the parts of the irrational nature through justice. . . . Above these are the cathartic virtues, which pertain to reason alone, withdrawing from other things to itself, throwing aside the instruments of sense as vain, repressing also the energies through

---

[†] By *irrational part* Taylor means that aspect of the human which is below the level of reason.

these instruments, and liberating the soul from the bonds of generation. . . . Prior to these [in the hierarchy], however, are the theoretic virtues, which pertain to the soul, introducing itself to natures superior to itself, not only gnostically, as some one may be induced to think from the name, but also orectically [*i.e.* through free will]: for it hastens to become, as it were, intellect instead of soul; and intellect, as we have before observed, possesses both desire and knowledge. These virtues are the converse of the political: for, as the latter energize about things subordinate according to reason, so the former about things more excellent according to intellect.

According to Plotinus,[7] there is also another gradation of the virtues besides these, *viz.* the paradigmatic. For, as our eye, when it is first illuminated by the solar light, is different from that which illuminates, as being illuminated, but afterwards is in a certain respect united and conjoined with it, and becomes as it were solar form; so also our soul at first indeed is illuminated by intellect, and energizes according to the theoretic virtues, but afterwards becomes, as it were, that which is illuminated, and energizes uniformly according to the paradigmatic virtues. . . . In what order, therefore, do the virtues first appear? Shall we say in the psychical?[†] For virtue is the perfection of the soul; and election and pre-election are the energies and projections of the soul. . . . [But of this paradigmatic species of virtue, Porphyry, in his *Auxiliaries to Intelligibles* writes

---

† Using psychical in its original sense, that is 'pertaining to soul.'

that they] are more excellent than the psychical virtues, and exist as the paradigms of these; the virtues of the soul being the similitudes of them.

To summarize, then, there are several levels of virtue which may be described as:

Physical and the *Ethical* which are shared with animals;

Political (or civic) which are exercised when the soul orders the irrational aspect of the mundane world;

Cathartic which are exercised when the soul liberates herself from generation;

Theoretic which are exercised when the soul looks to intellect as her model;

Paradigmatic which are exercised when the soul is entirely identified with the intellectual realm.

Heracles, as we have said before, represents the soul acting in the mundane realm, and we are not concerned, therefore, either with those virtues which are lower than the psychical (*i.e.* soul) order - the physical and the ethical - or those above it - the paradigmatic. Referring back to our exposition of the six worlds in chapter 2, page 12, and especially to the lower three worlds of matter, nature and soul, I suggest that the three middle levels of these virtues, the political, the cathartic and the theoretic, can be seen as the soul bringing rational order to each of the worlds. Thus:

By the *political* we order the world of *matter*;
By the *cathartic* we order *nature*;
By the *theoretic* we order *soul*.

But the nature of the soul is that it works through its faculties, which are principally three in number - the mind, the will and the heart. Platonic philosophers generally name these as reason, anger[†] and desire: they are concerned, respectively, with truth, goodness and beauty. When in a balanced and healthy condition the rational mind pursues truth and directs the will; the will pursues the good and, in turn, directs the heart; the heart pursues the beautiful and offers its object back to the reason for its further contemplation. Overarching these three faculties (which in the *Phædrus*[8] are symbolised by a charioteer and his two horses) is the unitive aspect of soul, which draws the separate activities of its faculties back into a coherent whole. Thus we can see operating at each of the three levels, four distinct virtues:

Prudence (or wisdom), by which the reason (or **mind**) is enabled to pursue truth and reject error;

Fortitude, by which the volition (or **will**) is enabled to pursue the good and reject evil;

Temperance, by which the desire nature (or **heart**) is enabled to pursue the beautiful and reject ugliness;

Justice, by which the soul (as a **unity**) is enabled bring the above three virtues into harmony and reject disharmony.

[†] The word 'anger' is used here to mean the faculty which imposes control on desires and actions. It has only a remote connection with the emotion we normally associate with the word.

One can see, from this simplified analysis of the virtues, that we ought to be able to see Heracles' labours in terms of Prudence, Fortitude, Temperance and Justice at three levels of activity. There are, of course, other ways to view the labours: in the *Shrine of Wisdom* Magazine a fine analysis appeared in issues 17 to 21 in which the twelve labours were aligned with the twelve zodiacal signs. It would be possible, too, I think, to find the correspondences between the twelve mundane gods and the labours. However we will follow our analysis of the labours in terms of the virtues. But one last set of correspondences might help us pick out which labour symbolises which virtue: at the level of political virtues we can be said to be ordering the cosmic aspects of ourselves and our environment; at the cathartic we are ordering the purely human aspects and at the theoretic we are ordering the divine aspects. We will see how, very often, these distinctions appear in the labours.

Generally speaking, the labours move in a circle which begins with a heavy involvement in the primordial creatures of early theogonies, passes through a more civilised phase, and then returns to the deeper deific reaches of the universe.

Labours I - IV, the Civic Virtues

The labours start with Heracles achieving mastery over the natural cosmic forces, which begin at a profoundly deep level: the Lion and the Hydra are monstrous offspring of primordial Gods, and, once vanquished, provide great powers for use in further and more difficult labours. From the Lion Heracles gains an impregnable cloak, which may be considered firstly as an indication that before terrestrial manifestation the soul gathers etheric and astral bodies which are more permanent than the gross physical body we are most conscious of, and, secondly, that once the virtue of civic fortitude is realised the soul cannot be distracted by external circumstances. From the Hydra, Heracles gains a powerful poison which greatly increases his power to vanquish his opponents and thus gain the objects of his quests. What does this tell us of the benefits of civic temperance? Temperance is that by which the 'heart' or the aspirational and desire nature is controlled and directed: without such control human efforts nearly always veer from one extreme to another and, in so doing, dissipate the drive towards the object of aspiration. The passage in Plato's *Phædrus*[9] concerning the chariot, especially the section which deals with the horse representing the desire nature, gives a fine exposition of the problems that intemperance presents to the soul.

I suggest that the quest for the Lion is symbolical of the unfoldment of civic fortitude, because of the lion's association with valour and because an important part of the volitional nature is to bring into actuality that which is envisioned; this faculty of will is concerned with *being* - and the skin of the lion provides Heracles with a body (*i.e.* an existence, the expression of being) by which he can traverse the world as a hero soul. Fortitude, then, is the virtue of the will (or, in Platonic terms 'anger'); the willingness of Heracles to lay down his weapons and use the more direct means of bare-handed wrestling is indicative of this initial virtue, and its primitive testing of the soul. A further interesting point is the need to drive the lion into a cave, before it will join in the wrestling match: the cave is a constantly recurring symbol of the material life in Platonic writing (cf. the *Republic*, and Porphyry's *Cave of the Nymphs*) - and, of course, the civic virtues cannot be exercised without the existence of the material world.

The symbolism of the Hydra labour as the unfolding of civic temperance is based on the fact that the myth is full of indications of the life-principle which is the basis of the soul's faculty of heart, or desire. The regeneration of the heads of the Hydra which have been severed, its name which is related to 'moist' and means water-serpent, its helper (the crab) emerging from the sea, and its immortal head, all seem to me to be sure signs that the Hydra stands for the dynamic power of life which must be accepted, assimilated and directed by the soul in its unfolding of temperance. The tale of the many heads growing in the place of one severed head is one of those truly vibrant images by which the ancient Greeks speak to us of the nature of ourselves and our environment: who can fail to be impressed by the way in which, in our material society, two desires spring up when one material desire has been assuaged? Athene, the Goddess of Wisdom, advised Heracles to cauterise each neck as soon as its head was severed: the properties of fire are symbolical of the way in which the fire of intellect can chose whether or not to allow a desire to grow in a particular place. The final motif - the burying of the immortal head beneath a stone -

perhaps shows us that the desire nature cannot be stilled entirely but when placed beneath something permanent - symbolised by the stone - will continue its work, without overpowering the whole life. Eventually, of course, the mortal life is yielded up by every terrestrial soul, and the problems which the blood of the Hydra brings to Heracles (as well as its benefits) are part of the final testing of the soul departing this earthly life.

We move now from the distinctly dark forces of the first two labours to the more natural forces of the remaining two of the initial group: The Erymanthian Boar provides the labour which allows Heracles to unfold civic prudence: the symbolism of using snow and a net to catch the beast is indicative of the use of the mind. Indeed Plato uses the analogy of a net when describing how a particular dialectic argument traps a character in the necessity of admitting a truth.[10] The coolness of the prudent mind - unswayed by the heat of passion - also mirrors the quality of snow. Once the virtue of civic prudence has been unfolded, Heracles joins the quest for the Golden Fleece, which is the quest for spiritual enlightenment. The hero is also required to subdue the half-man half-horse Centaurs, who represent, I think, the mind which is trapped in animal concerns (*i.e.* at the ethical level, which is below that of the civic) and who are inflamed by the fumes of wine, through which, as we have seen in chapter four, the soul is liable to be scattered into generation. It is after this labour, too, that there is the first intimation of immortality, when Cheiron is wounded and must find a mortal with whom to change places.

Finally the labour of the Keryenian Stag represents a completion of one stage: civic justice brings a comprehensive embrace to the civic virtues of fortitude, temperance and prudence. The comprehensive quality is symbolised in two ways in the myth; firstly, Heracles and the pursued stag move in a complete circle from Arcadia to the far lands of Hyperboria and back again; secondly the chase is timed over a complete year, so that the sun moves through every degree of its annual path. Such is the nature of the material world that the chase for material justice would go on forever, and so it is that Heracles uses an arrow to bring his quarry down. At this point the hero encounters Gods for the first time in his labours - Artemis and Apollo - and Heracles is, perhaps, shown the next level upon which he must work. Both Artemis and Apollo are concerned with the course of justice and the removal of injustice, and for this reason their respective myths appear, on the surface, to manifest a ruthlessness when wrong-doing is manifest - as we will see in chapter eight. Justice, at every stage, may be seen as the test of our entrance to the next level - if only because unjust situations left unresolved will always distract the soul seeking to unfold further works upon its path. Perfect balance is the key to Love's divine retreat.

I suggest, then, the following correspondences for the first four labours:

i) The Nemean Lion - Civic Fortitude.
ii) The Hydra of Lerna - Civic Temperance.
iii) The Erymanthian Boar - Civic Prudence.
iv) The Keryeneian Stag - Civic Justice.

Labours V - VIII, the Cathartic Virtues

The problems faced in this set of labours are, largely, those caused by human ills; three kings - Augeias, Minos and Diomedes - have neglected their duties and have created situations which require the intervention of the hero Heracles. The three primary instincts - self-assertion, self-preservation and self-expression - are symbolised by the Mares of Diomedes, the Stymphalian birds, and the Cretan bull (with the Augeian stables representing the wholeness of the instinctive nature). The task facing the soul who must unfold cathartic virtues is the removal of herself from the involvement with natural and instinctive impulses: that is not to say that these impulses are to be repressed, for this only leads to a more insidious involvement with them. Rather, the wise soul centres herself above the natural activities, from which position guidance can be maintained without submersion in the constant movement of the natural body. In most bodily activities which require a high level of co-ordination, the advice from experts is to keep the head still, as far as possible, and this may be translated into the cathartic virtues where the soul must find a place in which she may be still, while allowing the normal external activities to continue. The wonderful passage of Porphyry[11] sums up the need for detachment of those who aim to bring the soul and the natural body into right relationship:

> The soul is bound to the body by a conversion to the corporeal passions; and again liberated by becoming impassive to the body.

That which nature binds, nature also dissolves: and that which the soul binds, the soul likewise dissolves. Nature, indeed, bound the body to the soul; but the soul binds herself to the body. Nature, therefore, liberates the body from the soul; but the soul liberates herself from the body.

Hence there is a twofold death; the one, indeed, universally known, in which the body is liberated from the soul; but the other peculiar to philosophers, in which the soul is liberated from the body. Nor does the one entirely follow the other.

And, of course, Plato gives Socrates the words in the *Phædo*[12] which should stay with the philosopher at all times: "Those who are conversant with philosophy in a proper manner, seem to have concealed from others that *the whole of their study is nothing else than how to die and be dead.*" To which Olympiodorus adds,[13] "that *to die* differs from *to be dead*. For the cathartic philosopher *dies* in consequence of meditating death; but the theoretic philosopher is *dead*, in consequence of being separated from the passions."

The labour of the Stymphalian Birds is the exercise of cathartic fortitude, which is given subsistence by (as Porphyry, in his *Auxiliaries to the Perception of Intelligibles*,[14] says) "not fearing a departure from body as to something void and nonentity." Ares, as the God who especially calls forth the virtues (hence the shared root of Ares and Arete), figures frequently as a background player in these twelve labours, but in this particular labour is very clearly indicated: the birds are from his island; they are said to shoot iron arrow-like feathers, and iron is traditionally

Ares' metal; the wolves are also Ares-like animals, being noted for their aggressive hunting; the bronze rattle, too, is the harsh-sounding instrument which strikes fear into the opponent.   Against these birds Heracles had to contend, for by their numbers and their ferocity they were causing destruction to the region: his problem was their cover, the dark forest of Stymphalis, which is indicative of the way in which the normal instinct of self-preservation can cause an over-attachment to the material body. (The word in Greek which was often used to mean material, *hyle*, is actually the word for wood.) To solve the problem Heracles uses the rattle of Hephaistos which drives the birds back into their proper place, the air, and his own arrows which then caused them to depart for their home upon Ares' island. What does this mean? It might be worth pointing out that the rattle was, in the ancient world, associated with the worship of certain Gods: the sistrum is, for example, mentioned by Apuleius in the last book of *The Golden Ass*,[15] when describing the mystery cult of Isis. It may be that the myth is, in fact, an

extension of the mystery religions, whose primary object was to reveal to its initiates the true nature of life, and its continuance through the kingdoms of death. Whether or not this is so, we can certainly see that Heracles overcomes the fear that the birds had of the wolves by sounding a divine instrument which belittles the fear of merely natural

A sistrum of Isis

predators. Heracles, in common with these other cathartic tasks, retains nothing after the labour, but hands the dead birds into the keeping of Athene, who has enabled the hero to complete an otherwise impossible task.

The cleansing of the Augeian Stables, it seems to me, is the cathartic task *par excellence*. There are several interesting aspects which we should consider: the cleansing must be carried out in one day, and this indicates a singularity of activity - in other words the labour is not concerned with one of the several faculties of the soul, but the soul herself, which is the unifying principle of man. As such we can correlate the labour to cathartic justice, in which the whole cathartic life is harmonised and brought into unity. Porphyry's description of justice in this level of virtue[16] is "when reason and intellect are the leaders, and there is no resistance [from the irrational part.]" Heracles, according to Apollodorus, prepares for the double inundation by breaching the foundations of the stable in two places - above, where the water is to flow in, and below, where it will again flow out; thus there is no resistance when the waters of the rivers are channelled through the stables. The two rivers, by the way, are named after Okeanos who is, in the Orphic theology, the God of Separative Intellect. Heracles asks for payment for his labours, but, since this is a cathartic virtue being developed, it is not surprising that he leaves empty-handed. In some versions of the telling of the myth it is made clear that Heracles thinks the task is beneath him, and that is why he arranges things so that it is the power of the rivers which cleanses the stable rather than his own: and we see in this attitude the final lesson of catharsis - that the soul herself must not, if she is to act from her spiritual centre, become *involved* in the activities which are naturally unfolding in the mundane world.

One final point before we finish our consideration of the symbolism of this labour is the mathematics of it: the 3,000 oxen which have created the dung over thirty years can be analyzed into 3×10^3; the *three* represents the triple aspect of the soul (mind, will, heart, or reason, anger and desire) with which she energises when acting in the projected universe.   The *ten to the cubed power* represents the completeness of the soul projected into matter (for properly speaking there are only 10 numbers before the series repeats itself), for the single dimension is divine (and is not in existence), the square is the spiritual, and the cube is the material.   Thus the Chaldean Oracle says "Deepen not the plane" (*i.e.* don't extend the spiritual into material), as advice to the soul who wishes to rediscover the spiritual life.   Heracles asks, as a reward, one tenth of the oxen of Augeias, and this number (300) indicates that our hero is withdrawing from the deepened cube back to the plane (or square) - for 300 is 3×10^2. The time it has taken for the dung to build up is 30 years - 3×10, which may be seen, given the above reasoning, to indicate the hidden source of the triple powers of the soul.

The labour of the Cretan Bull is an unfolding of cathartic temperance; for the bull has always been taken as a symbol of the generative power which is the focus of the desire nature (the temptation of Minos is the desire to use the generative power of the bull among his own herd).   The whole episode has its origin in a bull rising from the sea - yet another symbol of the generation of life - and is completed, as far as Heracles is concerned, when it is driven back across the sea under his direction. The tragedy which unfolds in the myth of Theseus - the mating of the queen with the bull to produce a youth/maiden-consuming monster, housed deep in a labyrinth - also speaks to us of the problems when cathartic temperance is lacking. The insanity sent by the Gods in punishment of Minos' wrong-doing is actually received not by the king, but by his queen - again an indication that the life-generating principle of the royal house is at the centre of the crisis. So how does Heracles unfold this virtue? It is not by killing the bull - for that is not the path of catharsis - but by riding, in a directed manner, the instincts across their proper realm; once land is reached the hero releases the bull, for to hold on to it would have only moved the problems from one kingdom to another. A later hero, Theseus, who may well represent the theoretic life, is the one left to kill the bull and sacrifice it to the Gods - for, as Olympiodorus says,[17] "the theoretic philosopher is *dead*, in consequence of being separated from the passions." Heracles is quite satisfied, in his exercise of cathartic temperance, to have governed properly his quest animal. Porphyry[18] defines cathartic temperance as "not to be similarly passive with the body" and we can see that whereas the house of Minos is indeed passive with the body, to the point of mating with it (the bull being the largest domestic animal, its body being particularly impressive), Heracles rides *upon* it.

The labour in which Heracles tames the Mares of Diomedes unfolds cathartic prudence: the horse, being an animal long associated with the transport of man, is a symbol of the mind in all its aspects, by which the human

being may move swiftly from thought to thought.
Parmenides, when he describes his departure from mere
opinion-based truth to pure spiritual truth uses the image
of horses:

> The mares that carry me as far as my heart may
>   aspire were my escorts:
> They had guided me and set me on the celebrated
>   road.[19]

Again Porphyry describes cathartic prudence as "not to
opine with body, but to energize alone." Abderos (son of
Hermes, the God of the moving mind) whose name means
stupidity, may represent to us the opinionative faculty
which is forever bound to material concerns and is,
therefore, torn apart by his charges. But Heracles rules the
horses - again not by killing them but by feeding them
with their own master - and by this most subtle method
releases them to a higher realm (note here, too, the animals
are killed upon a sacred mountain, and not by Heracles'
hands). The lower mind is never still, but the soul must
develop that discipline by which she remains undisturbed
by its constant curiosity; by allowing the horses to feed
upon Diomedes (lit. 'God counselled') the myth indicates
to us that we may safely allow the lower mind to work
away at its own level - so long as the soul does not sink to
the level of opinion, but retains her place in the rational
and abstract realm.

We have now completed the cathartic virtues, and the
episode in which Heracles wrestles with Death lets us
know that the hero has passed through another initiation,
and is ready for his final tests. To summarise, I suggest,

then, the following correspondences for the middle four labours:

v) The Stymphalian Birds - Cathartic Fortitude.
vi) Augean Stables - Cathartic Justice.
vii) The Cretan Bull - Cathartic Temperance.
viii) The Mares of Diomedes - Cathartic Prudence.

Labours IX - XII, the Theoretic Virtues

The final four labours move Heracles into the realm of true soul activity, rather than the activity of soul through nature and materia: the prizes to be obtained in these quests are, mainly, those of divine origin. The labours take Heracles to the limits of the world, which indicate to us the boundaries of individual soul activity (there is, as we have seen in Plotinus' teaching concerning paradigmatic virtue, see page 119, a step beyond the projected universe which the soul may take - but here, strictly speaking, the soul is merged in the universal ocean of true being, and *in some respects* loses her individuality). The prizes, once obtained, are immediately passed on - in all but one case to the Gods (in all cases, if Admete as a priestess of Hera, is seen as the representative of that Goddess) - for these things are not possessions in the material sense, but are the means by which the qualities of soul are unfolded; such qualities are immediately radiated to those around that soul.

The Belt of Hippolyte was the gift of Ares to Hippolyte but was then required by Admete, a priestess of Hera.

This labour seems to me to be concerned with the virtue
of theoretic temperance, which Porphyry describes as "an
inward conversion of the soul to intellect." In theoretic
temperance, then, the heart or aspirational nature is used
to turn the entire soul into spirit (or intellect.) The
Golden Belt is held by Hippolyte whose name (lit. 'horse-
loosener') indicates that she symbolises the power of the
heart to release the intellect of soul, if we are to accept the
previous labour's interpretation; the Belt, a gift of Ares,
intensifies this power. The spiritual nature of the
Amazons is indicated, I think, by their name and most
commented upon practice: *Amazon* means 'without breast'
and ancient authors reported[†] that the Amazons "pressed
down" their right breast, so that their javelin throwing
would not be impeded. We can see, then, that the normal
operation of the breast - concerned with the nutrition of
those the mother has generated - is subsumed to needs of
the javelin throw. Now the javelin, like the arrow, is
often used as a symbol of desire, and especially the symbol
of higher aspiration, so that the Amazon can be seen as the
feminine energies converting to the higher realms: the
golden (or incorruptible) belt is to be taken by the hero
soul, and thus the power of conversion to spirit is

† The different authors used different wording to describe this
practice, concerning the right breast, the words here, "pressed
down," are those of Apollodorus at II, 5, 9. Some have interpreted
this as meaning that the breast was cut off, but it seems more likely
from Apollodorus' words that the right breast was bound tightly
to the body.

obtained. The passing on of the belt to Admete (lit. 'untamed') means that the feminine principle continues to rule its powers, and will continue to release the highest aspirations of the human heart. The queen of the Amazons, Hippolyte, recognises Heracles as worthy of being given the belt, and the whole transaction would have been accomplished without bloodshed had not Hera stirred up the war-like side of the amazons: a warning, perhaps, that if the heart is not properly informed of the truth it can cause division rather than union.

Theoretic prudence is defined by Porphyry[20] as "consisting of the contemplation of those things which intellect possesses." The capture of the Cattle of Geryoneus correlates with the virtue of theoretic prudence, or wisdom, for the entire story is centred around the two sun gods, Helios (the original God of the sun) and Apollo (who was the later Greek culture's God of the sun). Geryoneus was the son of Apollo, who himself kept cattle (and which were stolen by Hermes); Heracles follows the path of the risen sun, east to west, to come to the red lands of Erytheia; here, in the land coloured by the setting sun, even the cattle are red - and red is the colour of *being*, or that which intellect perceives;[†] the journey to the east is upon the barque of the sun. The sun, and the Gods Helios and Apollo, are rulers of the mind which casts light into

---

[†] The three primary colours are traditionally correlated with the three principles of being, life and intellect: intellect is yellow (or gold), blue is life, and red is being.

all regions, as Orpheus makes clear in his Hymn to Apollo:[21]

> O Delian King, whose light-producing eye
> Views all within, and all beneath the sky;
> Whose locks are gold, whose oracles are sure,
> Who omens good reveal'st, and precepts pure . . ."

Once captured, the cattle of Geryoneus give Heracles the same power as the sun to make things grow - cult centres and cities in this case - and to be aware of things even when asleep, so that the attempt by Cacus to steal the cattle fails. There are several details that we do not possess which, perhaps, would furnish more evidence for this correlation: the reason why Heracles should be set this task, and the origin of the cattle - were they divine? Certainly the dark cattle of Hades were kept nearby because their herdsman, Minoites, warned Geryoneus of the theft of the red cattle by Heracles. The defeat of the triple-bodied Geryoneus indicates the bringing back into unity of the many gnostic faculties of the soul, so that all things are seen with the single eye. The herd of cattle are taken through the world, exciting many men to attempt to steal them, but Heracles acts as the true herdsman, winning through many trials in order to bring the cattle to the altar of Hera; for all real intelligibles, although reflected in the material world, belong to the spiritual world, to which they always return. Geryoneus, by the way, means 'shouter' or 'roarer' - one who manifests the word, or logos.

Porphyry[22] describes theoretic fortitude as "apathy, according to a similitude of that to which the soul looks, and which is naturally impassive." The word apathy needs some explanation, as the modern translator might prefer such words as 'unmoving' or simple 'stillness' - but in this more accurate use of the word apathy consists in not being moved by any mundane consideration, and therefore allowing the soul to remain in the still point of the spirit. The capture of the dog Keberos is, I think, the labour which correlates to this virtue, for once the guardian of the boundary between life and death is lifted on to the shoulders of Heracles, the greatest of all changes that we experience - the movement between life and death - is eliminated, or shown to be a mere illusion. Heracles, by his entry into Hades, recalls to us, once again, the words of Olympiodorus,[23] "but the theoretic philosopher is *dead*, in consequence of being separated from the passions." We may recall, too, an early labour of the hero, when Heracles buried the immortal head of the Hydra under a stone: the shadow of immortality the hero discovers in his dealings with civic virtues is now revealed to be a premonition of the real immortality within the grasp of the re-spiritualised soul: the great truth taught to the initiates of Eleusis. The rescue of Theseus from these realms is also an indication of the power of the will of the soul when anchored in spirit; for the life force of the soul is, potentially at least, able to animate the deepest reaches of matter. The sacrifice of the cattle of Hades is the bringing of this life force into the darkness. The non-use of weapons in this labour perhaps indicates that the soul who exercises theoretic fortitude acts entirely within herself.

The final labour, in which the Golden Apples of the Hesperides are taken, represents the virtue of theoretic

justice: Sallust,[24] in writing on another myth suggests that
a golden apple represents the mundane world when he
writes:

> But we may perceive the mixed kind of fables, as
> well in many other particulars, as in the fable
> which relates, that Discord at a banquet of the gods
> threw a golden apple, and that a dispute about it
> arising among the goddesses, they were sent by
> Jupiter to take the judgement of Paris, who,
> charmed with the beauty of Venus, gave her the
> apple in preference to the rest. For in this fable the
> banquet denotes the supermundane powers of the
> gods; and on this account they subsist in
> conjunction with each other: but the golden apple
> denotes the world, which, on account of its
> composition from contrary natures, is not
> improperly said to be thrown by Discord, or strife.

Now we have already indicated that the virtue of justice
conjoins and harmonises the other three, and here we have
the last labour bringing as one prize the three golden
apples which may be considered as the perfected virtues of
theoretic temperance, wisdom and fortitude, or,
alternatively as the three projected worlds of soul, nature
and matter (now properly comprehended by the theoretic
soul) which constitute the mundane realm in its widest
sense. Theoretic justice, which Porphyry defines as
"performing what is appropriate in a conformity to, and
energizing according to intellect" is indicated in this labour
by its being performed according to the advice of
Prometheus, who, as we have before suggested, is the
divinity who carries the deepest intellectual energy into the
mundane realm, and who is, as Olympiodorus says[25] "the

inspective guardian of the descent of rational souls. For to exert a *providential energy* is the employment of the rational soul, and, prior to any thing else, to know itself." Justice, in which heart, mind and will are brought into balance, is the great pre-requisite for knowledge of one's self. Once the soul has unfolded the virtue of theoretic justice, she ensures that the order ordained by Zeus is restored (thus Atlas was tricked into resuming his task, having served the purposes of Heracles). The Golden Apples, too, are replaced upon the tree which stands in the blessed isles of the west, to which the soul returns when her labours are complete.

We have come, then, to the end of all the labours of Heracles; and the divine gifts of the last group of tasks are returned to their rightful places. It now remains for Heracles to enter the Olympic realm, having burnt out the mortal part of his self, by the exercise of his great strength, and by the proper sacrifice in fire to his father, the mighty Zeus. The image of Athene leading Heracles to his place among the Gods was, not surprisingly, an often repeated one among the artists of the ancient world. To summarise the correspondences of the last four labours, I have suggested the following:

ix) The Belt of Hippolyte - Theoretic Temperance
x) The Cattle of Geryoneus - Theoretic Prudence.
xi) Keberos - Theoretic Fortitude.
xii) The Apples of the Hesperides - Theoretic Justice.

The twelve labours can, then, be set out in tabular form, as given in table 1.

Faculty and virtue:	Heart Temperance	Will Fortitude	Mind Prudence	Unity Justice	
Civic level:	Hydra of Lerna	Nemean Lion	Erymanthian Boar	Keryeneian Stag	*(soul looking down)*
Cathartic level:	Cretan Bull	Stymphalian Birds	Mares of Diomedes	Augean Stables	*(soul looking within)*
Theoretic level:	Belt of Hippolyte	Keberos	Cattle of Geryoneus	Apples of the Hesperides	*(soul looking up)*

Table 1: The Labours of Heracles & the virtues.

Notes

1. The myths of Heracles are drawn 1) concerning his conception, from the *Ehoiai* and the Homeric epics; 2) concerning his infancy, Ps-Eratosthenes, and Diodoros; 3) concerning his early exploits Apollodorus, and Pausanias; 4) concerning his labours, Apollodorus and Diodorus.

2. *Odyssey* 11, 269.

3. *Inscriptiones Graecae* 14, 1293 D.

4. See *The Shrine of Wisdom Magazine*, nos. 17 to 21.

5. See Taylor's collection of Oracles, TTS vol. VII, p. 11.

6. See p. 309, TTS vol. XII.

7. *Ennead* I ii 7, TTS vol. III, p. 177.

8. *Phædrus*, 246a ff.

9. *Phædrus* 246a - 256d; especially 253e - 255a.

10. The *Sophista* 235b.

11. *Auxiliaries to the Perception of Intelligibles*, I, 7 - 9 [TTS vol. II, p. 170].

12. *Phædo* 64a.

13. In his Commentary on the *Phædo*, 3.1.

14. *op. cit.* 11, sect. II, 34. The three following comments from Porphyry are also to be found here.

15. *The Golden Ass* XI, 11, 4.

16. *op. cit.* 11, section II, 34.

17. Olympiodorus' Commentary on the *Phædo*, III, 3.

18. *op. cit.* 11, section II, 34.

19. Parmenides 28. b1.1 f.

20. *op. cit.* 11, section II, 34.

21. Orphic Hymn XXXIV, TTS vol. V, p. 83.

22. *op. cit.* 11, section II, 34.

23. Olympiodoros' Commentary on the *Phædo*, III, 3.

24. Sallust, *On the Gods and the World*, IV; TTS vol. IV, p. 7.

25. Olympiodorus' Scholia on the *Gorgias*, see TTS vol. XII, p. 427.

Chapter Seven

Athene

Gathers herself together through the help of Apollo
And the saviour Athene, by truly purifying philosophy;

The line of Damascius couples Athene and Apollo as the paradigm of the souls return from the realms of incarnation. We will consider Athene first, for reasons which will become apparent in the suggested interpretation.

The Myth[1]

Of all the spouses of Zeus, Metis is perhaps the most mysterious of all. It was said that she was equal in wisdom and courage to the Thunderer himself; indeed, some say that she "knew more than all other Gods and men." The daughter of Okeanos and Tethys, Metis had given Zeus the poison which had rendered Kronos sleepy, and by which the son had been able to force the father to yield up all the devoured brother and sister Gods of Zeus. Metis was able to shape-change so that when Zeus pursued her, the chase consisted of a series of metamorphoses, until the God finally coupled with this most wise Goddess.

Now Gaia and Ouranos warned Zeus that from Metis would be born to him a daughter and then a son who, if he should arise, would overthrow his father's kingship - just as Zeus had overthrown Kronos before, and Kronos had overthrown Ouranos before him. To prevent such an eventuality, Zeus tricked Metis and swallowed her whole. After a while Zeus complained of a headache, and Hephaistos - or according to some,[2] Prometheus - took an axe (or hammer) and split the Father's head, at which point we will turn to the beautiful Homeric Hymn to tell the tale:

> Zeus the counsellor himself bore Pallas Athene from his august head. Clad with golden and resplendent warlike armour, as awe lay hold of all the immortal onlookers. And before Zeus the aegis-holder she sprang swiftly from his immortal head, brandishing a sharp-pointed spear. Great Olympus quaked dreadfully under the might of the grey-eyed goddess, as the earth all about resounded awesomely, and the sea moved and heaved with purple waves. The briny sea calmed down when the splendid son of Hyperion stopped his fleet-footed horses long enough for maidenly Pallas Athene to take from her immortal shoulders the divine weapons. And Zeus the counsellor exulted. And so hail to you, O child of aegis-holding Zeus!

All this took place on the banks of the river Triton, from which she is given the name *Tritogenia*.

There is a suggestion that Zeus bore Athene, acting as both father and mother, in response to Hera bearing Hephaistos without the assistance of Zeus (it is unclear if Hera generated him alone or with another father).

Athene (or Athena) was commonly known as Pallas Athene (Pallas can be, according to inflection, male or female in Greek, meaning either strong youth or strong maiden), and there are many differing reasons suggested for her assuming this name: there is a shadowy God named Pallas, who could be an alternative father - although it has to be said that the constant reference to Zeus' relationship to Athene makes this a rather peripheral supposition. A more easily assimilated story is that Athene grew up with a playmate called Pallas, with whom she would practise battle games; one day Pallas aimed a blow at Athene and all-seeing Zeus feared harm to his daughter and so parried the blow with his aegis. As Pallas' aim was deflected Athene delivered her attack and, off balance and defenceless, the playmate took the full force of the strike - and so perished. Athene made a wooden statue of her to preserve her memory, and also took her name.

Pallas Athene was known as the Virgin Goddess - thus the name of her great temple upon the Acropolis at Athens, the Parthenon. This virginity was never threatened - a rare thing in Greek mythology - except upon one occasion: Hephaistos, as a reward for acting as the axe-wielding midwife in the birth of the Goddess, demanded from Zeus that Athene should be his in marriage. Zeus giving his blessing, Hephaistos pursued Athene who first fled (giving the lame God a very hard task to catch her), and then, when caught, fought off her would-be husband in the moment of sexual embrace. In some versions she actually vanishes in the middle of intercourse. As a result the seed of Hephaistos did not enter Athene's virgin womb but fell on the earth, from which Gaia gave birth to Erichthonios, whose sacred precinct stands next to the Parthenon. Despite this, Athene seemed to accept responsibility for this child and having received him from

Gaia, the Goddess put him in a basket and placed it in the keeping of the three daughters of Kekrops, king of Athens. She tells the three princesses not to open the basket - a request that seems impossible to keep in the world's myths and folk-tales - and not unnaturally curiosity overcomes the keepers. Variations exist as to the consequences of this act, but it is clear that one or more of the daughters see either a child enwraped by a serpent, or a half-child half-serpent creature (Erichthonios had a serpent lower half according to most reports) and was sent mad by the sight. One, two or three of the princesses leapt over the steep face of the Acropolis to their deaths. This is not the place to go into details of the subsequent life of Erichthonios, except to say that he is the traditional founder of the Panathenia - the great festival which was the focus for the cult of Athene as the guardian Goddess of the City of Athens.

Athene is associated with the aegis which is a protective cloak, and with the spear (see plate 6) - both of which she was born brandishing. The aegis was said to have been made by Metis, and to cause battle-fear when it was rattled (it seems to have had metallic tassels woven into it). The colour of Athene's eyes are worthy of remark, although different translators give them as grey, blue, azure, and green; she was called 'owl-eyed' and, indeed, the owl is constantly assigned to her as her emblem.

The Goddess presides over many areas of activity: with Ares she rules war (and, when confronting him seems to have had the better of the exchanges), and was known as Atryone, 'the unwearied one.' With Hephaistos she governs crafts, especially metal work; with Aesklepios she rules the healing arts. She is also the patron of domestic skills, and especially weaving; one of her names is Kaliurgos, the 'maker of beauty,' and her skill in weaving the peplos was celebrated as the central ritual in the Panathanaic festival. But, of course, Athene is primarily known as the Goddess of Wisdom, and the worthy daughter of All-seeing Zeus and Metis, the Goddess who 'knows more than any Immortal or mortal.' One of her cults was of Athena Pronoia (or Providence), and the remains of her sanctuary in this aspect just outside the Delphic Sanctuary of Apollo are still to be seen.

From these governing powers, it is to be expected that the Virgin Goddess is a most beneficent deity: stories of punishment of mortals by Athene are very few. Three exceptions to this are the blinding of Tiresias, who appears in many dramas as the blind seer, with whom Athene grew angry when he saw her naked; Arachne, who boasted that she could weave better than the Goddess and was changed into the creature who now bears her name; and Ornytos, who was cursed with a wasting sickness after he had wounded her in the thigh. Generally, however, she was revered as the saviour Goddess, and recognised as the great friend of mortals - her gift of the olive tree to Athens persuaded the citizens to yield to her the protection of the City, rather than Poseidon, who had caused a salt-water spring to appear on the Acropolis.

It is her patronage of Heroes, however, which is most striking; we have already seen that Heracles was helped on several occasions by Athene. Others who the Goddess

aided include: Jason, to whom she gave a figure-head of
sacred oak to affix to his argo - the oak was from Dodona,
and was, therefore, oracular; Belophantes, to whom (after
he had slept in her sanctuary) she gave the bridle which
facilitated the capture and taming of the winged horse
Pegasus; Theseus, to whom she appears as an adviser in a
dream; Tydeus, to whom she offered immortality, until his
savage behaviour prompted her to withdraw the gift, with
the consolation that it would be bestowed upon his son
Diomedes. (Diomedes is given particular attention by the
Goddess during the siege of Troy - she it is who allows
him to wound Ares.)

One further hero to whom Athene gave help is Perseus,
whose quest to defeat the Gorgon was accomplished with
the help of the Goddess: it was Athene, together with
Hermes who guided Perseus to the three sisters, the Graiai,
who shared one tooth and one eye. By stealing the eye
and tooth, the hero forces the sisters to reveal the
whereabouts of the Nymphai, who possess Hades' cap of
invisibility, the winged sandals, and the magic *kibisis*.
Once these are obtained both Hermes and Athene
accompany Perseus to the lair of the Gorgons, and warn
him that he must look away as he decapitates the gorgon;
they also tell him which of the three gorgons is mortal.
Athene holds a polished bronze shield up so that her hero
can accurately strike the blow by which the gorgon called
Medusa is beheaded. Perseus puts her head, the face of
which petrifies men, into his kibisis, and flees from the
remaining (immortal) gorgons: Athene also helps in this
last stage of the quest, ensuring that, even though Perseus

is invisible, there is no chance that he will be caught. This scene of flight is a favourite of ancient artists. Athene is often depicted as bearing the gorgon's head upon her armour or shield, and is sometimes called *Gorgopis,* 'gorgon-faced.' A further tale, following this episode, is the gift Athene gave Asclepios - the blood of the gorgon - which if drawn from the left side of her body was a deadly poison, but if drawn from the right was an antidote even to death itself.

Athene is one of the three Koric (virgin) Goddesses, the other two being Persephone and Artemis. She was also one of the three Goddesses who were subjected to the judgement of Paris - Aphrodite being judged the most beautiful in preference to Athene and Hera - which was to lead to the epic siege of Troy. In this story the Gods were at feast when Eris, or Discord, appeared and threw a golden apple into the midst of the banquet: the ownership of the apple was then claimed by the three Goddesses, and Zeus decreed that whichever of them was adjudged the most beautiful by Paris would win the apple. Each Goddess promised Paris a reward (Hera offered rulership, Athene wisdom, and Aphrodite the beautiful Helen): Paris, in electing Aphrodite, was enabled to abduct the wife of Agamemnon, and thus caused the conflict between the Greeks and the Trojans.

This brings us to the most significant myth as regards Damascius' analysis in which Athene figures: the story of Odysseus. We have already listed some of the heroes patronised by the azure-eyed Goddess, but Odysseus is by far the most favoured by her. Athene figures prominently

in the *Iliad*, the first of Homer's two major epics;[†] here
she is mainly seen in her capacity of warrior maid - her
philopolemic aspect. She is firmly on the side of the
Greeks (remembering that the Trojan Paris has, by his
judgement, placed himself and his city beyond the direct
beneficence of Athene); she balances the aggression aroused
by Ares who inspires the fighters of Ilium (Troy). But it
is in the *Odyssey* that she takes the leading role, providing
by far the most important divine intervention and
inspiration of the epic voyage.

Odysseus, of all the Greek heroes of the siege of Troy,
was the most reluctant to join the expedition, for Homer
reports that he alone was aware of the long exile (ten
years) the revenging army was choosing as its destiny. He
was also the man, once embarked upon the siege, most
faithful and useful to the Greek cause: it was his craft
which finally broke the stalemate, using the famous ruse of
the wooden horse.

After the city of Troy had been taken, the Greeks began
to prepare to return to their homeland; but this return was
not to be a happy experience for many of the victors -
Agamemnon's homecoming, for example, was quickly
followed by an inglorious death at the hands of his wife

[†] I realise there is some debate as to whether the same person
actually wrote both the *Iliad* and the *Odyssey*; but I think once the
differing purposes behind the two halves of the one story are
understood, it will be seen that the stylistic differences, which have
led certain modern scholars to question the authorship of the
double epic, are necessary to the unfoldment of these purposes.

and her lover, who had usurped the king's bed while he laid siege to Ilium. Others, too, perished in sea-wrecks. Odysseus, together with his followers from Ithaca, set out in three ships with the intention of making directly for their long unseen home: but this was not to be, and the journey home, during which Odysseus lost every single companion, was fated to take the same length of time as the siege of Troy itself. Many were the adventures set to try the strength, cunning and patience of Odysseus: the lure of the lotus eaters, the dread cave of the Cyclops, the anger of the king of the winds, the attacks of the giant Lestrigons, the enchantment of Circe, the descent into the infernal regions, the sirens, the twin dangers of Scylla and Charybdis (faced twice), the storms brought about by the fury of Hyperion, and the long half-happy, half-sorrowing exile of the isle of Calypso. Once these trials were faced, and the followers of the king of Ithaca were destroyed, Athene pleaded his case before her father, the King of the Gods; it was she who reminded him that Odysseus was lawfully fated to return home; it was she who convinced Zeus that he should send Hermes to command Calypso to yield the hero to his homeward journey.

Now Odysseus sets out from the island of the nymph Calypso; Athene rescues her champion from Poseidon's mighty storm, and arranges a friendly reception for him in the land of the Phæancians, who are to provide the thought-swift ships which at last deliver the hero back to his homeland. Meanwhile, the Goddess had rallied Telemachus, Odysseus' son, to plan against the suitors who had laid siege to the palace of the long-lost king (a curious inversion of the siege of Troy) and remove him from the harm they might do him; further, she had ensured that Penelope, his wife, also had the wisdom and heart to resist the suitors. All these things were done by the Goddess in disguises and dreams.

But now that Odysseus sets foot once more in his own kingdom Athene appears before him in her divine form letting her disguise drop away with the words "And yet you did not know me, Pallas Athene, Daughter of Zeus, who always stands by your side and guards you through all your adventures." Revealed, she speaks her words of counsel to him in the Cave of the Nymphs; Goddess and hero together, sitting upon an olive tree, now plan the actions which bring the hero back to his full estate, casting her power of illusion upon Odysseus himself so that his identity is concealed from the suitors. After some while battle between the gang of suitors and Odysseus with his son ensues, in which Athene joins in support once again of the hero. This has the desired effect, and the Royal house of Ithaca is purged of unlawful suitors, and, after the reconciliation of old feuds is effected, the awesome power of the Goddess brings peace to Odysseus' kingdom.

Greek Names

Athene, according to Plato (*Cratylus* 407b) is derived from θεο *divine* and voe *intelligence*.

Metis, signifies thought, or counsel.

Tritogenia means 'born from the Triton' - which has three possible connotations: it can mean that Athene was born on the banks of the river Triton; it could refer to her birth from the principle of water, since Triton is a general term for the presiding divinity of water; it could refer (as strictly speaking she is said to have been born from the peak beside Triton) to her birth from the head (peak) of Zeus, who, in the order of intellectual Gods, succeeds Rhea - the flowing intellectual life giver.

Pallas is a reference to the rhythm and movement - vibration, if you like - of dance, again according to the *Cratylus*.

Erichthonios may be derived from Eris, *dispute*, and Chthonios, *Earth*, as he was conceived in the earth, as a result of a dispute between Athene and Hephaistos. It is somehow pleasing to see that the famous marble decorations of the Parthenon, or 'Elgin Marbles' which depict the procession said to be founded by Erichthonios, are still exercising their power and causing a long-running dispute between the British and Greek authorities!

Perseus 'son of Zeus.'

Odysseus has an interesting root, according to Liddell and Scott, of δυς, which is a prefix like our un- or our mis- as used in unrest and mischance; they say it always has a notion of "hard, bad or unlucky." From this we can see that Odysseus stands for the soul in the extremity of material existence, who must struggle with ill-fate and who longs to flee from such a life.

Suggested interpretation

Zeus is the great Intellectual Creator of the projected universe, the Demiurgus - lit. the 'worker of or for the people' - the so-called second creator (as The One is the originator of the entire universe, inner and outer, and is therefore the first creator).   But Zeus is the Creator because he remains entirely focused upon the intelligible realm and does not move into his own creation; this is the task of his offspring.   But of his offspring there must be one who is as close to the paternal pattern as is possible under these circumstances: and this is Athene, who is an unmixed reproduction of the Father.   Whenever we meet with Gods swallowing Gods we must consider it to be an attempt in mythological terms to convey the idea that one divinity includes another in terms of him or herself - that the swallowed god is occultly held within the depths of the swallower.   Thus Metis is the counsel which is held within the depths of Zeus, and which springs fully formed from the highest aspect of the Creator in the guise of Athene. This Goddess, then, is the leaping forth of the Divine Mind - the providential gift of truth to those creatures of the projected universe capable of receiving reason.   The idea that had Zeus produced a son from Metis he would have been overthrown suggests that another God would have come forth to project another complete universe *within* Zeus' universe - an unnecessary replication in some senses, and yet exactly what happens *in miniature*, once the rational soul has unfolded its powers of creative thought.

There is a tradition which says that a twin which survives the death of its partner in the womb in some mysterious way carries that partner's spirit throughout its life. We can, perhaps, apply this romantic idea to Athene, who does not have her prophesied brother, and yet seeks to make every earth-born soul grow to the stature of a heroic demigod, who rules his or her own microcosm. Her male-female characteristics confirm that she carries both sister and brother of the Zeus-Metis coupling.

From the moment of conception, then, Athene is an integration of two apparently opposing forces. All the domains of the Goddess can be seen as means of reconciling opposing or complementary movements; war is the most outward reconciliation of contradictions: two sides have different aims at the beginning of war, and fight until one aim (not necessarily either of the originals) dominates the parties. Wisdom is a more comprehensive and inward reconciliation of opposites - here the different forces of the individual, society or environment are brought into a viable balance. Health, too, can be seen as a balance between the various physiological and psychological energies within an organism. Even weaving is the balancing of the tensions of the woof and warp.

In her dealings with heroes we may safely assume that Athene brings about a balance. But what is the balance between?

The great problem for the incarnating soul is to reconcile its inner spiritual nature and impulses with its outer nature and desires. Further, this reconciliation cannot be a compromise - for merely to trade the extremes of one kind of life and consciousness so that the middle ground is gained, diminishes the power and comprehension of the soul. No! This retreat into mediocrity will not work, and the human spirit rebels whenever it finds itself trapped in such a luke-warm situation. Some way must be found to be entirely spiritual and entirely corporeal. Does this sound like an impossible task? But that is what every hero is meant to face.

The first arc of Campbell's circle is the outward moving one, in which the trials of mundane life are faced and overcome. It is an arc of increasing dominion over the lower forces of the universe, but one, paradoxically of increasing limitation. Whenever the human being sees an area of endeavour in the mundane world he or she must either put 'heart and soul' into it, or fail to gain the full reward of its movement within that area. If the individual goes into any major enterprise believing the thing to be an illusion, that individual will undoubtedly fail to put the necessary thought and effort into it to properly succeed. The late Bill Shankley, the extraordinary manager of Liverpool Football Club is often quoted as having said that "Football is not a matter of life and death - it's much more important than that!" This may have been at least some of his secret of success. Now the hero, in his quest for the golden fleece, the holy grail, the apples of the Hesperides, or whatever, must be convinced that the object of his quest is all-important. But herein lies the danger, for the obtaining of any object in the mundane realm - no matter how full of symbolic spirituality it may be - is in itself nothing compared with the true spirit which *is*, and which *is without process.* In gaining the prize, the soul may lose herself.

Athene, the Goddess of wisdom, will always help the questing soul who is descending the arc of terrestrial life in pursuit of some worthy aim. But her unique providence is in the gift of flight, by which the mundane object is transformed or transferred into the realm of spirit; there are many surviving statues of Athene in which she is represented as being winged. Thus it is that Athene leading Heracles to Mount Olympus was a popular artistic theme in ancient times; and, also, the depiction of Perseus in flight with the Gorgon's head aided by Athene is a powerful one.

Most of the mythological themes surrounding Pallas Athene can easily be understood in the light of the power of wisdom to spiritually transform the hero and his prize, so that he or she may begin the return to the homeland.

We must now turn to the story of Odysseus and consider it in this light. For a more detailed analysis of Homer's work, Thomas Taylor's *Select Works of Porphyry* is certainly worth reading, for in it Taylor not only translates Porphyry's beautiful *On the Cave of the Nymphs* but also adds his own extensive *On the Wanderings of Odysseus*.

The traditional neoplatonic view of Homer's *Iliad* and *Odyssey* is that the former epic deals with the soul's pursuit of the reflection of Spiritual Beauty in the material world: Helen represents this Beauty which is stolen from its proper emplacement in the eternal realms (symbolised by Greece) and taken to the foreign world of earth (Troy, or Ilium - from the Greek word for mud). The ten year siege

represents the entire microcosmic experience of the
mundane realm, only successful when the Greeks place
themselves into a sacrificial body - the wooden horse
(remember the word hyle means both *wood* and *matter*,
and by extension *material world*). The taking of Troy
represents the perception of the spiritual beauty in the
mundane, and is another expression of the exertions which
we have considered in the chapter on Heracles. Indeed,
many writers actually give Heracles just ten tasks as the
proper series undertaken for Eurystheus, since the cleansing
of the Augeian Stables was part of a mercantile
arrangement and therefore disallowed by Eurystheus, as
was the slaying of the Hydra because Heracles was assisted
by Iolaos. A variation on the Homeric telling of this story
grew up in classical times in which Helen was said to
reside in Egypt during the siege, and that the Greeks and
Trojans fought over only her phantom - an image, rather
than reality - which fully conforms to the Platonic teaching
regarding the relative realities of the eternal and transient
realms.[†]

[†] The opening of speech of Helen in Euripides' *Helen* has the
following passage, in which she explains her presence in Egypt:
"But Hera, indignant at not defeating the goddesses, brought to
naught my marriage with Paris, and gave to Priam's princely son
not Helen, but a phantom endowed with life, that she made in my
image out of the breath of heaven; and Paris thought that I was his,
although I never was, - an idle fancy! . . . for Hermes caught me up
in the embracing air, and veiled me in a cloud; for Zeus was not
unmindful of me; and he set me down here in the house of Proteus
[in Egypt]."

The *Iliad* then, is the myth of the downward moving soul which must go through the stages of the rape of Persephone, the scattering of Dionysus, and the chaining of Prometheus, and arrive at the tasks of Heracles - no wonder then, that the tale is one of masculine hardship and battle. The *Odyssey*, on the other hand, according to the neoplatonists, is the tale of the returning soul, moving from the tasks of Heracles, through Athene-assisted flight, back into the true homeland of the hero. It presents a progress from the hardships of unfolding the virtues in the mundane world, to that of the point of perfect peace in which the soul's spiritual activity is unimpeded.

The *Odyssey* has a curious presentation of time: all the tasks which correspond to the Heraclean phase (*i.e.* to the point at which Odysseus leaves the island of Calypso) are set in the past. All these tasks have exercised the virtues of Odysseus in relation to the world; the hardships have reduced his possessions to nothing - all the plunder of Troy is lost, all his companions are gone - he just has himself. Through the first major intervention of Athene he leaves the island and Homer begins his 'present tense phase' - that is to say he has moved into relations to what has been called 'the eternal Now.' Odysseus sails across the ocean for nine days and nights, during which time he does not sleep, but keeps his eyes upon the guiding stars - a motif of spiritual awareness - and arrives, with one last test from Poseidon, Lord of the ocean of generation, upon the shores of Phæatia completely naked. Here Athene's intervention is again called upon, and the long-wandering hero is received by a people who represent beings of true intellect, who travel the seas on 'ships of thought-speed' and who give to the man they recognise as a king gifts of great beauty and value. Thus the material gifts lost in the ocean of Poseidon are replaced with spiritual gifts which are the birthright of every soul, if only she is receptive of them.

Now Odysseus had been reluctant to leave Ithaca, for he had the foresight to see what weary trials lay in wait for him once joined in the Greek expedition; but like a true hero he had treated the enterprise with his utmost efforts and brought about the success of the siege. However, Athene's path is one of catharsis, and Odysseus had, in his wanderings, taken the Goddess' antidote to the illusion of material reality in full measure. By this means the profundity of wisdom is revealed to the hero, who is permitted to sit with his Goddess. What remains to be done is to take up the bow of Apollo and reduce the suitors to nothingness - and therefore leave just one king of the Kingdom of Ithaca. We will see in our suggested interpretation of the myth of Apollo how this is really a perfect representation of the God's characteristic activity.

Odysseus' reputation as a liar suggests that he is speaking spiritual truths which appear to be lies to those whose only point of reference is that of materiality.

The night-hunting owl is a symbol of the powers which the soul unfolds in her flight from the dark world of matter to the light of heaven. The love of wisdom, which is the meaning of the word philosophy, is the means by which our soul's eyes are opened and become as perceptive as those of the owl.

The initiation of Athene asks the question "how are my achievements to be offered up to the Gods?" Or perhaps more profoundly, "how is my now truly active self to be offered up to the Gods?" The answer that wisdom provides to these questions means that the hero soul avoids the trap of over-identification with effects rather causes; she ensures that mystical effects continue to be generated long after we ourselves have turned our outward attention from our achievements.

Notes

1. The myths of Athene are drawn from Hesiod's *Theogony* (conception); the Homeric Hymn to Athene, no. 28 (birth); and the numerous references to her in both the *Iliad* and the *Odyssey*, and Apollodoros' *Library*.

2. Apollodorus I, 3, 6.

Chapter Eight

Apollo

*Gathers herself together through the help of Apollo
And the saviour Athene, by truly purifying philosophy;*

The Myth[1]

We have already touched on certain elements of the myths concerning Apollo - he has been seen as defending his prophetic place at Delphi from the designs of Heracles, as well as commanding the hero with regard to the Hind of Keryneia, and has played an important role in the central myth of Dionysus. We now turn to the complete corpus concerning Apollo, as far as it survives.

Apollo was the son of Zeus and Leto, the daughter of the Titan Ciois; he was, it seems, a twin, although Artemis his twin sister acted as midwife during the birth of Apollo, so we must either accept the miracle of a minutes-old baby being a midwife, or consider that at some point Artemis and Apollo were merely sister and brother. Before the birth of Apollo, Leto had wandered the world seeking somewhere suitable to be the birthplace of this most important God who, says the Homeric hymn "is to rule over all mortal men." Eventually Leto, after speaking to the spirit of Delos, a rocky and barren island, agreed that this previously neglected place would receive the child Apollo. Many Goddesses attended the birth, which started unexpectedly early and went through a phase of labour of nine days and nights before Eileithyia, Goddess of Birthing, was sent for: jealous Hera had persuaded her to remain on Olympus, and Iris with the gift of a necklace nine cubits long, was given the task of spiriting Eileithyia away to where she was needed in Delos. When she set foot on the island the Goddess brought the labour to its proper pitch and, in the words of the Homeric hymn "Apollon sprang forth to the light." (An alternative timing of his birth is, however, suggested by one of his names which means 'born on the seventh day'.²) Themis poured him ambrosia and nectar and immediately upon receiving them Apollo threw off the swaddling of babyhood and spake: "My wish is to hold dear the lyre and the curved bow and to prophesy for men the unerring will of Zeus" - with this Apollo walked away over the earth and its wide roads. He wandered the world looking for a place to establish a temple and his cult-worship. Eventually he came to Delphi, at the foot of mount Parnassos, where a terrible python-shaped monster held sway - this was the daughter of Hera who, outraged at Zeus bringing Athene to birth without the help of a mother, brought forth her own fatherless offspring. Apollo overthrew her and brought to the spot (under the guise of the form of a Dolphin - hence the name *Delphinius*) a crew of Cretan sailors to act as his priests in the Delphic Sanctuary. It is interesting to note, however, Apollo's words to Telphousa, the female spirit of the spring of the region: "The glory of this place will be mine, too, not yours alone." Certainly the feminine roots of Delphi, with its first divinity being a fatherless daughter of the Queen of the Gods, were maintained, so that the priestesses of the Sanctuary rather than the priests were those who spoke the oracle of the God, and held the greatest renown throughout the world of the Hellenes.

We have seen how, at his birth, Apollo claimed for himself the lyre, the bow, and prophecy; we must look more closely at those areas which the ancients considered his domain. One of them was certainly music - he was *Musagetes* 'leader of the nine muses' - and he received from Hermes the gift of the first lyre as a peace-offering after the child-God had been exposed as the thief of Apollo's herds of cattle. He killed Linos for attempting to rival his musical talents, as well as Marsyas who competed with Apollo's lyre using a flute which had been thrown away by Athene (because it disfigured her face). This last rivalry was decided when Marsyas, who had claimed to match anything Apollo could do on the lyre, was finally undone by Apollo playing his lyre upside down - an impossibility with the flute. As it had been agreed that the winner could choose his prize, Apollo decided that he would claim Marsyas' life; the mortal died by being suspended from a high pine tree and being flayed alive. Of the three great musician-prophets of Ancient Greece, Hesiod dedicates his work to the Muses, but Homer certainly claims the guardianship of Apollo, and Orpheus was said to have ended his life, having laid out the rites of Dionysus, as a priest of Apollo. Pythagoras, too, the great advancer of musical theory, was associated strongly with Apollo.[3]

Apollo, with his sister Artemis, were the wielders of the curved bow - he was known as the 'far-shooter.' Apollo also bore a golden sword: both these weapons have distinct symbolic relations with the sun, whose golden rays penetrate the furthest corners of the world, filling all things with light. By classical times Apollo was associated with the sun, having taken over the rulership from Hyperion. Both Artemis and Apollo were not reluctant to use their arrows; for example they shot Tityos when he attempted to ravish Leto, and, following Niobe's boast that she was better blessed than Leto with children, the Goddess shot all her female children, and the God shot all her male children. Apollo was known as Phoebus (which means holy light) because of his association with brightness, and it is by this name that Shakespeare invokes him in *Cymberline* -

> Hark, hark, the lark at heaven's gate sings,
> And Phoebus 'gins arise,
> His steed to water at those springs
> On chaliced flowers that lies . . .

Of his prophetic powers we have several mythological episodes to underline the high regard with which Apollo was held by the ancients: Melampous met the God on the banks of the river Alpheios, and was taught the art of divination by inspection of sacrifices, becoming "the best of diviners from that day forth." More dramatic was Apollo's relation with Cassandra, the princess of Troy, with whom he fell in love: he wooed her with the promise that he would teach her prophecy, but once learnt, she reneged on her agreement and rejected Apollo. He then gave her a further gift (being unable to take back his first), which was the curse of never being believed when she announced her prophecies. In the Dionysus-Titan myth, of course, Apollo used his prophetic powers to warn his half-brother of his impending doom, but in this case was ignored. A very late story (from Virgil) has the Cumaean Sybil being given a thousand years of life by Apollo - but because she refused his advances he did not give youthfulness without which a thousand years of life is a fairly hideous prospect.

One less well-known attribute of Apollo was his rulership of herds - he originally held a 'shining whip' by which herds were marshalled, but exchanged it with Hermes for his lyre. When Apollo killed Cyclopes for having made Zeus' thunderbolts, after one had been used to destroy his son Aesklepios, he was sentenced to serve Admetos for one year as a herdsman.

Another aspect of Apollo is bringer of justice - again this may be traced from his light-giving qualities, for justice exposes the evils committed under the cover of darkness. An example is from the Orestian Trilogy in which Apollo commands Orestes to avenge the death of Orestes' father, Agamemnon, who was killed by his wife and her lover on his return from the siege of Troy.

Apollo was also closely associated with healing, and this was passed on to his son, Aesklepios, who was borne by Koronis until Apollo heard of her unfaithfulness: at which point he asked Artemis to kill the mortal but snatched the child from her womb as she died. The bringer of the news of Koronis' infidelity was a raven - one of Apollo's symbolic animals - which was originally white but changed

to black by Apollo in his anger at the news. But Apollo's
relation to healing is not a simple one, in common with
many other of his attributes, and he was equally well
known as the bringer of plague.

We have already briefly mentioned the Oedipean or
Theban Trilogy in connection with Dionysus; but in this
classical period drama Apollo has a pivotal role to play.
Very briefly, it is the Oracle of Apollo which continually
brings about the exceptional circumstances of the tragedy;
it prompts the parents of Oedipus to expose the child at
birth; it prompts Oedipus, having been saved from such a
premature death, to flee his adopted Corinth and, in
ignorance, return to the kingdom of his birth, Thebes; it
is the Oracle to which his father is journeying when
Oedipus slays him; it is the Oracle which prompts
Oedipus, by now king of Thebes, to investigate the
circumstances in which he has unwittingly found himself.
While the appalling results of all this are extremely
Dionysiacal in character - the son killing the father,
marrying the mother, and, later, brother killing brother,
and uncle entombing his living niece - the last of the three
plays of the Theban trilogy to be written, *Oedipus at
Colonus*, brings Oedipus in an almost ritual drama to the
rest "promised by Apollo." The tragic king's death, he
himself says, is to be a "holy mystery that no tongue can
name" and, amid peals of thunder, he leads his small
retinue towards the appointed place, despite his blindness.
He goes before the hill of the harvest goddess (Demeter)
and removes his clothing, which is stained through many
years of toilsome wandering across the face of the earth;

once washed and purified, he dismisses all but Theseus, king of Athens, and "by a swift invisible hand he was lifted away to the far dark shore." The chorus pray that "Out of the night of his long hopeless torment surely a just God's hand will raise him up again."

Greek Names

Apollo, 'a' the negative, 'pollo' meaning many - in other words Apollo means 'not many' - which is a good definition of 'one'. Some recent scholars (Walter Burkett, for example) have suggested a more obscure derivation of the name, which, they say, comes from a phrase meaning 'he of the assembly'; this is, at least superficially, at variance with Plato's explanation in the *Cratylus*, of 'not many'. However it may be that with some thought the two explanations are not so far removed if we think of 'he of the assembly' as meaning 'he who makes the many parts [of the assembly] into one'.

Leto (or Latona) is derived, says Plato in the *Cratylus* at 406a (and Proclus in his commentary on it), either from 'smoothness' or from 'voluntary' - for she is the mother of the God who brings culture and the self-chosen life.

Artemis, says Plato in the *Cratylus* at 406b, signifies integrity and modesty; Orpheus, says Proclus (in his commentary on this passage), identifies Artemis with Hecate.

Suggested interpretation

It was Pindar who stated that Apollo and Artemis were twins - the characteristics of each are very similar and support Pindar's assertion - although more ancient authors merely call them brother and sister. If we need an explanation as to why a twin acts as a midwife to her partner we might consider the ancient assertion that 'Zeus and man created man' - or, in other words, that Zeus created the arche, or principle, of man and that this arche then generated all the subsequent aspects. This can either be taken to mean that there is an unbegotten Archetypal Man from whom all individual men are derived, or that each soul has a head which is the direct creation of God, from which all else is self-generated. The *concept* of twins being in some sense one entity and the *image* of one twin acting as midwife to the other combine to suggest this mystical 'generated and at the same time self-generated' doctrine.

Certainly, the indication is that Apollo must be viewed as the ruler of the objective world in its fullest manifestation, for he himself says that to him it falls to announce the unerring will of his father, the Creator Lord Zeus, to all mankind, and the Homeric hymn says he is to rule over all mortals. The Hellenic world recognised Zeus as the maker and father of the world and, as such, possessing a primacy in the ruling Gods, but saw Apollo as his intervening representative and, therefore, very often referred to simply as 'the God.' Christianity has made us familiar with the idea of 'god made flesh' or 'son given to the world' and, while this is not as far as the Greeks would have gone, the combined characteristics and mythical adventures of Dionysus and Apollo can be seen as the expression of the principle manifested in other myth-cycles as Christ, Krishna and Osiris. Apollo is often represented as riding a swan (see plate 7) - a bird symbolic of the soul in the myths of the Greeks, the Hindus and the Celts.

The question of the time of Apollo's birth (born on the seventh day, or the ninth) may be considered as reflecting his creative progenitor - for the creative activity of Zeus is sevenfold; or it may be considered as the first expression of the God's relationship to the one-and-manyness which puts him as 'leader of the nine': in numerology there are nine numbers (or ten, if the mysterious zero is added), beyond which the numbers really just repeat themselves in higher terms. Starting at the number one the number sequence progresses until, having reached nine, unity returns as 1 with 0, which is 10. The nine muses, or the powers of art and science unfolded, are brought into a unity by the addition of Apollo, who is the tenth of the musical figures.

Upon his birth Themis - Goddess of Law - feeds the child ambrosia and nectar, which represents eternal being and life, and immediately the pure light which is Apollo walked over the earth and its wide roads: all the attributes of Apollo - rulership of music, prophecy, the golden far-darting arrows, healing, justice, divine herdsman - can be seen as contributing to the return to integrality of wandering mundane souls. It is through this symbolism that we must view his absolute ruthlessness in so many of his myths. The slaying of Tityos, Marsyas, Niobe's children, Linos and others is, in reality, the reduction of multiplicity back into oneness: the story of Marsyas is, perhaps, the most striking example of this. Marsyas takes as his favoured instrument the very one which Athene, Goddess of the wisdom of flight from illusion, has discarded; the flute distorts the face (a detraction from the proper beauty of the player, taken very seriously by high-born Greeks)[4] and which relies on the outward movement of air from the player across the sounding hole - reminiscent of the way in which the Platonists saw the path of the soul into materiality, via the pneumatic body. The lyre, on the other hand, does not distort the musician and allows words to be sung by him while he plays - and thus the word, reason or *logos*, maintains its place within the musical harmony. The characteristic of the soul is that it is a unity, and as such has no up nor down, left nor right; the lyre being playable in any position is allied to the soul in this respect, while the flute, dependent upon position, represents body which is a complexity of parts. Apollo wins his contest with Marsyas because of the superiority of his instrument - the soul over body - and, having won, suspends the loser on an evergreen tree (again representative of the immortal soul) and strips off the outer layers of the failed musician, thus starting the process which every returning soul must undergo, that of reduction to essential simplicity.

The herdsman, of course, brings a multiplicity of animals into a oneness - that of a single herd. Apollo gives his shining whip to Hermes in exchange for the lyre, and this must suggest to us that the mechanics of the herding of souls towards their spiritual home is delegated to Hermes - as is indicated by an epithet of Hermes, *psychopompos* 'leader of souls'.

Dionysus, as God of the descending horizon (see page 73) is abducted by piratical sailors in his myth which deals with the separating aspect of the soul's path. Apollo, in contrast, as God of the ascending horizon, abducts trading sailors to furnish his sanctuary with a priestly line; he is collective where Dionysus is separative, and he rules over, where Dionysus is (temporarily) ruled over.

Apollo has a very ambiguous relationship to sexual union - hardly surprising since this union (which in itself might be considered as Apollonical) brings about generation and multiplicity. Apollo's rejection by so many mortal women and nymphs, either in immediate rejection or by subsequent unfaithfulness, tells us, I think, that the God is not concerned with the generation of new forms, but rather the assimilation of many forms into oneness. The raven, in this respect as a carrion bird, is properly considered his since it reduces that which is dead to its skeletal form. Damascius draws our attention to the words of Socrates in the *Phædo*, when he says that the aim of the true philosopher is to die and be dead: these are two distinct states since *to die* is a process of passing from life to death, while *to be dead* is a stable state. The soul which is under the leadership of Apollo has already passed under the aegis of Athene, whose wisdom enables the soul *to die*. Her bird - the owl - is a hunter - its victim undergoes the process of death; but Apollo's bird - the raven - deals only with those animals who are already dead.

We have mentioned before that the great mystical leaders of Greek thought - Homer, Orpheus, and Pythagoras - claimed discipleship of Apollo; it is interesting to note that Socrates in his death cell, spent his last night composing hymns to Apollo (as instructed in a dream) and that his last words were to remind a disciple that a cock should be sacrificed to Aesklepios, Apollo's healer son. The cock, as a bird which greets the sunrise, was considered by ancient commentators to be a solar bird.

Apollo's rulership of healing is clearly a further effect of his characteristic activity of restoring wholeness, or integrality; his son, Aesklepios, further distributes this activity, although he dies by the thunderbolt of Zeus because he cured those who had died. The whole question of life and death, health and ill-health is a complex one: Socrates, in the second phase of the *Phædo* suggests that *all opposites that are characterised by process are productive of each other*. He goes on to show that (mortal) life produces death, and that death produces (mortal) life; Apollo's association with plague as well as with healing is, perhaps, a recognition of this fact. Plagues, which were primarily the problem of cities, served a purgative purpose amongst the living organisms which were the ancient cities. Aesklepios' crime was to intervene in the natural cycle of life and death by which the soul learns its most valuable lessons: a warning, I feel, for our present death-fearing civilisation!

Finally we should consider the dramatic rendition of the initiation of Oedipus at Colonus. The story of Oedipus is the story of the problem of material manifestation for the soul: Oedipus is clearly an intelligent man - he answers the riddle of the sphinx - but the complexity of cause and effect, with its numerous hidden traps, defeats his attempts to live the just life. This is really the condition of most of us, for the vast majority of mankind would like to live according to the Good, but cannot discern its path through the highways and byways of mundane life. Oedipus is shown his failings in the starkest possible light and this man who has won his kingdom (properly his by birthright) through reason ends the first of Sophocles' plays by blinding himself: he thus turns his attention from the outer world to his own inner world. One might see this as symbolising the Athene stage of 'flight', and certainly the fact that the remaining years of his life are lived following the steps of his unmarried daughter, Antigone, would seem to indicate that he has thrown himself on the mercy of the virgin spirit of the Goddess. Now at Colonus, where his wanderings across the earth have led him, he is to take the final step and leave even this guidance behind. The second play is centred around the sacred grove of the 'Kindly Ones' (Eumenides) - the Furies - who drive souls to their just ends. Having taken sanctuary at their shrine, Oedipus hears the sounds of thunder and lightning which Apollo has promised as a sign that the much-troubled king will find his final rest. (It is interesting to note that the thunder and lightning are the very same accompaniments to the scattering of souls into this world, as given at the end of the tale of Er in the tenth book of the *Republic*;[5] these signs, it seems, indicate the opening of the gates between this world and the next.)

Once Oedipus has resisted the last attempt by its new ruler to force him back to the city of Dionysus (Thebes) to act as perpetual talismatic protector of its borders - in other words to be tied to the world of duality - he is ready to be elevated by Apollo.   Now that the final stages of the purification of the Athene-led stage are completed, Oedipus removes his earth-stained garments and washes himself, and his ability to pick his own path is returned despite, or perhaps because of, his blindness.   The voice of the God now speaks directly to him, in just the same way that Athene spoke directly to Odysseus at the end of his journey.   The final act of Oedipus' life is unseen by mortal eyes, as only Theseus (his name means 'son of God') is permitted to remain to the end; his going is reported by a messenger whose final words show us that this Apollonic initiation is beyond ordinary understanding:[6] "Certain it is that he was taken without a pang, without grief or agony - a passing more wonderful than that of any other man. *What I have said will seem, perhaps, like some wild dream of fancy, beyond belief. If so, then you must disbelieve it. I can say no more.*"

   The soul's Apollonical initiation is, as in other myths, indicated by death; the unbearable sadness of separate existence is only thus removed.   This initiation asks how we are to find our simple unity amid the multiplicity of powers, energies and achievements, which as hero-souls we have made our own.   By it we are prepared for an assimilation to the perfect Henads, or ever-loving Gods.

Notes

1.   The myths of Apollo are drawn mainly from the Homeric *Hymn to Apollo* (III); also used are several references to him in the *Iliad*, the *Ehoiai*, the Homeric *Hymn to Hermes* (IV), and Apollodorus' *Library*.

2.   *cf. Works and Days* 770, where it is maintained that Apollo was born on the seventh day.

3.   See Iamblichus' *Life of Pythagoras*, TTS vol. XVII, p. 204.

4.   cf. the *First Alcibiades*, 106e; see also the accompanying note to this passage in TTS vol. IX, p. 180.

5.   cf. The *Republic* 621b.

6.   *Oedipus at Colonus*, 1660.

Chapter Nine

Demeter

And she elevates herself to the causes of her being
with Demeter

The Myth[1]

Demeter, sometimes called Deo, was the daughter of Kronos and Rhea, born second after Hestia according to Hesiod, and was, therefore, consumed by Kronos because of the warning given to the God by Ouranos and Ge (or Gaia) that an offspring of this union would overthrow Kronos. When Zeus forced Kronos to disgorge his brothers and sisters, Demeter emerged to take her place amongst the Olympians.

Demeter's rulership is of the harvest: her symbol, which appears again and again in ancient art, is the wheat stalk; to her the blood sacrifice was more often than not set aside, the sacrifice of the first fruits of the field being preferred. It was said that her two great gifts to mankind were primarily the mysteries, and secondarily grain. One of the main celebrations of Demeter in Greece was the festival of Haloa; this name is derived from the word meaning threshing-floor, although it took place in December, long after the season for threshing had passed. We have seen how the main weapon Demeter used to force the return of her daughter was the withdrawal from the world of her powers of ripening, so that no food was available to man or beast. There is a local myth of Attica mentioned by Pausanias which has Demeter giving the fig tree to Phylatos because of his hospitality to her.

One largely neglected myth has come down to us from Kallimachus which tells of a prince, one Erysichthon, who led twenty of his servants to a sanctuary of Demeter in order to cut down its sacred oaks. To prevent this the Goddess took the guise of her priestess, Nicippe, and ordered the prince to turn away from his task; he refused, and looking at the priestess with "eyes like a fierce lioness" vowed that the trees would be cut down to make a great well-roofed house in which he would feast. Then Demeter, taking on her true form, replied "So, so, build thy hall, thou dog, thou dog, wherein thou mayest hold banquets: for frequent festivals shalt thou have hereafter." And with this she visited on Erysichthon an insatiable hunger, which brought ruin of abject poverty and disgrace to him and his family. No more appropriate punishment could be imagined for those who show impiety to the Mother of grain.

The greater part of the surviving myth of Demeter is concerned with the Persephone abduction, to which we will return shortly. Demeter had three sexual liaisons recorded by our extant myths: the first is a short but unambiguous statement in Hesiod that Zeus came to Demeter's bed to father Persephone; according to Orphic tradition this coupling took place when both parties were in the form of a serpent. She is also raped by Poseidon during her search for her lost daughter; to avoid him she transformed herself into a mare, but Poseidon took the form of a stallion and so Demeter gave birth to Areion, a stallion, and a daughter whose name, according to Pausanias, "shall not be repeated by the uninitiated." This unwanted liaison with Poseidon made her angry and hence she was worshipped in Onkion as Demeter the Fury; here two statues held pride of place - one of the Goddess holding a basket and a torch, and the other of her washing. Nearby there was a cave sanctuary to 'Demeter the black', a reference to her mourning clothes she wore during this time. The third sexual encounter of Demeter was with Iasion, reported by Hesiod thus: "Demeter, bright Goddess, was joined in sweet love with the hero Iasion in a thrice-ploughed fallow in the rich land of Crete, and bare Plutus, a kindly God who goes everywhere over land and the sea's wide bank, and he who finds him and into whose hands he comes he makes rich, bestowing great wealth upon him." Calypso complains, in the *Odyssey*, that Zeus struck Iasion with a thunderbolt in retribution for this liaison.

Demeter, of course, means Mother Goddess and apart from giving birth to Persephone, her maternal aspect was also recorded in a myth fragment which says that she had pity on Plemnaios whose children all died with their first breath: she came to him disguised as a foreign woman and brought up Orthopolis (his next son) herself to ensure his survival.

We must now turn again to the story of the abduction of Persephone, but look at it in terms of the resulting actions of Demeter. This is how the Homeric hymn records her first reaction to the loss of her daughter:

"Bitter pain seized her heart, and she rent the covering upon her divine hair with her dear hands: her dark cloak she cast down from both shoulders and sped, like a wild bird, over the firm land and yielding sea, seeking her child. But no one would tell her the truth, neither god nor mortal man; and of the birds of omen none came with true news for her. Then for nine days queenly Deo wandered over the earth with flaming torches in her hands, so grieved that she never tasted ambrosia and the sweet draught of nectar, nor sprinkled her body with water. But when the tenth enlightening dawn had come, Hecate, with a torch in her hands, met her, and spoke to her and told her news."

Hecate, who some say was also Demeter's daughter, reported that she had heard Persephone's cry as she was stolen away. Hecate and Demeter went to Helios and were told the identity of Persephone's abductor. We have several variations available here, including the possibility that Triptolemos, son of the King of Eleusis, brought Demeter the news of Persephone's descent into Hades.

Once she is told of Kore's fate, Demeter shuns the company of the Gods and descends to the world of men - the 'eaters of grain' - and comes to the land of Eleusis. Here she sits by the Maidens' Well, where the women of the royal house of Eleusis were accustomed to draw water. The four daughters of King Keleos ask her to care for their infant brother Demophoon and Demeter agrees, giving herself a false history of having escaped after being abducted by pirates from a home in Crete - she calls herself Doso. This agreement being ratified by the queen, Metaneira, Demeter begins her godly nursing of the child, anointing him with ambrosia and placing him in the embers of the fire every night. We have seen in chapter three how this attempted process of converting Demophoon into an immortal is interrupted by his mother: this method failing however, Demeter, now revealed as a Goddess, commands that a temple should be built to her honour and in which she may teach the Eleusinians her rites. Some versions have it that Triptolemos, not Demophoon, was the recipient of Demeter's failed gift of immortality; more certain than this, though, is the tradition that Triptolemos was the first initiate of the mystery rites of Demeter.

During her sojourn in the house of Keleos, Demeter was, as one might expect, solemn and unlaughing: to lift her bleak mood a servant, Iambe, entertains her with some kind of mockery - from which a tradition sprang in Attica that at certain festivals the women would gather and honour the Goddess by ribald joking. A variation on this episode reported by Clement makes her a guest of Dysaules and Baubo, the latter, finding the disguised Demeter gloomy, pulled up her skirt and exposed herself to the Goddess, much to the Goddess' delight. During her stay at Eleusis Demeter refused to drink wine but provided a concoction of barley-meal, water and pennyroyal. On the subject of diet, Pausanias remarks on a shrine to the 'Bean Man' near Athens, saying "I am not sure if he was the first to grow beans or they simply named a hero like that because the discovery of beans cannot be traced to Demeter. Those who know the mystery of Eleusis will know what I am talking about."

Following her stay in Eleusis, Demeter then withdrew entirely from mortal and immortal company, bringing a year-long barren period, while she abided in her shadowy temple.   Zeus, failing in a plan in which Iris would persuade Demeter back to her normal activities and providential care of the harvest, finally sent Hermes into the depths of Hades to bring Persephone up to Olympus, while Rhea spoke to her daughter setting out the perpetual scheme whereby the stolen bride would spend a third of the year in Hades and the remainder upon bright Olympus.   This being agreed, the harvest once more moved in its accustomed cycle, and Demeter spread her mysteries amongst many kings of men - "awful mysteries which no one may in any way transgress or pry into or utter, for deep awe of the Gods checks the voice. Happy is he among men upon earth who has seen the mysteries; but he who is uninitiated and who has no part in them, never has lot of like good things once he is dead, down in the darkness and gloom."

Greek Names (See also chapter three).

Hecate, 'far-shooting'

Rhea, 'flowing'

Kronos, pure intellect from 'kore' and 'nous' according to the *Cratylus*; alternatively the name may be related to 'chronos' meaning time.

Deo, simply 'goddess'

Doso, 'freely given'

Suggested interpretation

According to Plato,[2] the name Kronos refers to pure intellect (it being a corruption of kore-nous); we may certainly understand him as the first Intellectual God who, rather than creating from the intelligible paradigm set up by the Intelligible Gods of Being, is solely concerned with the contemplation of the paradigm. He is the 'static' God, who does not proceed into creativity; thus all his progeny are immediately swallowed, and, therefore, they do not proceed outwards into expression. But Rhea, whose name means 'flowing' is the proceeding intellectual Goddess, whose gift is the life which empowers the intellectual creation of the projected universe. Thus she conspires to prevent the permanent subsumation of her children conceived with Kronos and, when Zeus is born, gives Kronos a rock instead of the baby God, hiding her child in a cave in Crete under the care of the Curetes, the intellectual guardian Gods. Zeus is the last of the three great intellectual deities, who is 'idealising' or creative: that is to say he takes the intelligible paradigm and creates its perfect and ideal reflection - mysteriously converting the paradigm of the highest Gods into an offering to the One. To Zeus, then, the task falls to release the hidden and subsumed powers that Kronos holds within himself; the now matured Zeus emerges from his childhood cave and gives to his father a poison provided by Gaia which forces Kronos to regurgitate his children. Having caused their second births it is fit that Zeus is called the 'father of Gods' even though, clearly, he is not the first father of all

the Gods. We may view Zeus as father and creator of the
projected universe, and the Gods and Goddesses he brings
forth as the ruling divinities of the universe. Demeter
being one of these is, in this sense, a child of Zeus, but to
complicate matters she is also his sister, and to further
complicate them, she is identified as Rhea, Zeus' mother,
in the Orphic theology: can we get any more complicated?
Yes, for in the same theology Zeus mates with Rhea-
Demeter to produce Persephone. Thus Demeter is the
mother-sister-wife-daughter of the Creator God, and is
especially concerned with the proceeding into life by the
soul. Greek writers often distinguished between the
various kinds of beings by referring to their food: the Gods
were those that ate ambrosia (literally this means 'not
mortal'); humans were the eaters of grain and meat; and
animals the eaters of grasses. Demeter, then, is clearly the
mother of those mortals who are the eaters of her grain,
her best-favoured sacrifices. In Proclus' *Theology of Plato*
Rhea is named as the 'fountain of souls'† but since some
souls are not partial, and therefore do not descend -
properly speaking - into generation, it is as subsisting
within Demeter that she is the fountain of partial souls -
and thus the giving birth to Persephone is symbolic of the

---

† ". . . . we must say that soul and intellect are established in
him [Zeus] exemptly; and that Zeus participates of both these, from
the Gods that are prior to him; of intellect indeed, from his father,
but of soul from the queen [Rhea] who is the deity of vivification.
For there the fountain of soul subsists, just as in Kronos, there is
intellect according to essence." (V, 24)

entire generation of human souls, or those souls whose path to life is through the realms of death.

This path is one of movement between realms, as we have seen, and the soul's learning is intimately bound up with the process of growing and diminishing; putting on clothing, so to speak, and removing it; affirming truths and denying the unnecessary accretions which then gather around them. The business of the threshing floor is the removal of the inedible useless husk which holds the vital grain - an image of the very experience suffered by the soul which descends into generation: the celebration of the Haloa may well have revealed this truth to its participants.

Of course every human soul, being endowed with free-will, has the choice of remaining entirely involved with the manifested cosmos, or of discovering her spiritual essence: whatever the choice, Demeter gives her vivifying power. Erysichthon ignores the sacred and sees Demeter's trees as useful mundane building materials: his twenty servants are reminiscent of the Pythagorean doctrine that the twenty-sided icosahedron represents the element water, and the assertion of Porphyry that 'moist' souls are those descending into generation. This being the case Demeter visits upon the prince the insatiable appetite of which all natural things participate. The true mystic, however, hungers for the real food of the highest realm, for as the Chaldean Oracles say,[3] "The intelligible is food to that which understands."

We have already looked at the implications of the Demeter-Zeus mating, but what of that of Demeter-Poseidon? One of the problems of unravelling the relationships of the Gods is that very often one name serves as a reference to two or more levels of subsistence of a God. This is certainly the case with Zeus, the name we give the intellectual creator of the projected universe; but also the name we give to the creative deity of the liberated order of Gods, and to the similar god of the mundane order of Gods. As the Creator, Zeus is the Demiurgus; but as a liberated God he is one of the three Demiurgi, Poseidon and Hades being his brother Demiurgi. Here Zeus is given rulership of the sky, Poseidon the oceans, and Hades the underworld. Poseidon as ruler of the ocean is father of flowing generation (thus his role as opponent of Odysseus' flight from these realms to the spiritual homeland). Demeter, coupling with Poseidon, produces a stallion son - the horse representing the mover of men through the world - and a daughter "whose name cannot be mentioned except by the initiated"; who is this? Orphic theology says that Hecate was the daughter of Demeter, and she is very often linked with Persephone, although more generally thought of as an independent 'Goddess of the Underworld'; I would suggest that Persephone and Hecate are two aspects of one Goddess: Persephone is the soul who is born of an intellective father, Zeus, while Hecate is the soul born of a liberated father, ruling the flowing kingdom of nature. Persephone, therefore, is recalled to Olympus, the mountain of Intellectual light and seat of Zeus, while Hecate remains as the ruler of the lower kingdom of life-in-matter. Plate 8 shows Triptolemos being initiated into the mysteries by Demeter while Hecate stands at his shoulder.

Demeter's liaison with Iasion in the 'thrice-ploughed' field would seem to be a reference to the mysteries, the highest initiates being taken through three initiation rites, and thus becoming elevated to union with the mother Demeter; from such a union true wealth of soul follows, since Demeter is the Goddess of fruitfulness. Those who are so initiated are liable to be struck by the power of Zeus, by which means they are converted to the intellectual heavens.

The search for Persephone by Demeter includes the aid of Hecate and if we are to see Persephone and Hecate as closely allied, it is interesting to note which one is lost, and which is able to join in the search: Persephone, the offspring of the intellectual father, is lost in the darkness of matter, since to the intellectual being the world of matter is confusing and unintelligible, at least at first. Hecate, however, daughter of the ruler of generation is, far from being lost, able to help search through the world, because her essence is not so foreign to matter.

We see that Demeter refuses ambrosia and does not wash during her searching: thus she shows her providential care of mortals who have not arrived at that state in which they can partake of immortal food, and who are immersed in matter. This idea of Demeter's providential nature is more fully indicated by the name she gives herself at the Maiden Well, Doso, for this name is derived from the word meaning 'given freely.' Certainly all Demeter's actions at Eleusis are providential, for her first action is to attempt to impart immortality to the child of the royal house of Eleusis, and then, when that fails, to instigate the mysteries which impart immortality in their own deeper ways to all who present themselves at the sanctuary. The ribald remarks of Iambe and the episode in which Baubo exposes her organs of generation to the Goddess cause divine laughter - for the Goddess of immortal life cannot but be amused by the idea of sexual reproduction, which Diotima in the *Banquet*[4] shows to be a weak attempt at ensuring immortality.

The symbolism of grain is in its dying and regenerating in the spring: Demeter refuses wine during her search for her daughter because it is the symbol of Dionysus who is scattered by generation, but produces a mysterious mixture which is grain-based.

Demeter withdraws her ripening powers from the world once she finds that Persephone is held in dark Hades: she herself retires into her temple in Eleusis. By this stratagem she forces the return of her daughter. Of her two gifts, grain and the mysteries, she chooses to withhold the lesser - that which nourishes the mundane body - in order to recover her daughter, who represents the soul. Thus the world dies in its first winter and is born again to the spirit when Persephone is returned in the first spring.

It is worth remarking that although Demeter searches the world with her torch, she does not descend into Hades once the whereabouts of Persephone is revealed; instead it is left to Hermes the messenger of Zeus (sometimes called the dæmon of Zeus) to negotiate and guide the return of the daughter.

By the counsel of Rhea, Demeter is reconciled to the order of things whereby Persephone is of both the upper

208741t worlds. Thus, too, we see the Orphic
identification of Demeter with Rhea, which is something
that I am convinced Damascius had in mind when
composing his verse; for as we have said, Rhea is the
fountain of souls, and in being "elevated to the causes of
her being with Demeter" the soul is returned to the source
of her intellectual-life, which is occultly held within
Demeter.

Demeter rules seed and fruit. The fruiting phase of any
plant or animal is the phase in which the mature organism
is no longer energising for its own good but for the sake of
future generation; this is the 'elixir' stage of Campbell's
cycle, in which the returned hero puts to work the prize
he has gained in the other world for the sake of his home
world. This is an all-important final step: in the Heracles
stage the soul saves the world because of her actions, but
in *this* stage she saves the world because *she is*. The end of
all her struggles is peace, and in the soul's peace she
becomes god-like; the words of Proclus[5] in describing the
providential stillness of the gods have rarely, if ever, been
bettered:

> For the Gods do not govern all things either by
> investigating what is fit, or exploring the good of
> every thing by ambiguous reasonings, or by looking
> externally, and following their effects as men do in
> the providence which they exert on their own
> affairs; but pre-assuming in themselves the measures
> of the whole of things, and producing the essence of
> every thing from themselves, and also looking to
> themselves, they lead and perfect all things in a
> silent path, *by their very being*, and fill them with
> good.

In the Heracles phase the soul works upon substances external to herself, and by process. In her elevation to Demeter the soul works only upon her own substance, and without process. It may seem to our worldly eyes that the most powerful things work upon things other than themselves; this is not so: the most powerful work only on themselves and in so doing have an unlimited effect on other things.

The final initiation of the soul, her return to Demeter, is the pure revelation of her unific self, beyond the limitations of multiplicity: through this initiation she rests at the centre of the universe, as does a sun at the centre of its solar system, providentially radiating light, warmth and power.

The soul in returning to Demeter reaches the Mother-Deep, of which Lao Tsze says:

> The spirit of the Void never dies.
> It is called the Mother-Deep.
> The opening of the Mother-Deep is called
>   the Root of Heaven and Earth.
> Ceaselessly, ceaselessly,
> It nourishes and preserves:
> Inexhaustible, without effort.[6]

May all the powers of Heaven and Earth guide you back to the Mother-Deep.

Notes

1. The Homeric *Hymn to Demeter* (II) is the chief source of Demeter's myth together with Hesiod's *Theogony*; references to her are used from Apollodorus, Pausanias, and Kallimachos' *Hymn to Demeter* (VI), and the *Ehoiai*.

2. *Cratylus*, 396c, more fully unfolded by Proclus in his Scholia on the dialogue at 107 to 108.

3. See page 24, *Oracles and Mysteries*; The Prometheus Trust, Frome, 1995.

4. *The Banquet* 207c - d.

5. *Theology of Plato*, I, 14.

6. The *Tao-Teh King* of Lao Tsze, Shrine of Wisdom translation, p. 18.

Chapter Ten

Some Conclusions

And from thy fables, mystic and divine,
Give all her powers with holy light to shine.
Proclus' Hymn to Athene

We have travelled the cycle of Damascius' verse - perhaps just in words, perhaps in thought, and perhaps even in some inner experience. I hope the reader will have had some glimpse of those mysteries in which the beginnings and endings meet. I must repeat that the explanations I have given are only suggestions - the start, I think, of a golden thread in our common labyrinth - and that I am certain that many more precious truths remain hidden in these myths for the reader to find in his or her own quiet moments.

I would like to offer one more analysis for consideration: we have looked at the circle of the soul's journey as divided horizontally, but we can also divide it vertically. In this division we may consider the downward moving arc of the circle as that of the lesser mysteries, which Thomas Taylor says, in his treatise *On the Eleusinian Mysteries*,[1] are concerned with the soul invested with a earthly body, merged in a material nature, suffering purgation and trials, and undergoing lives and deaths. The ultimate goal of this arc is to accomplish the Heraclean initiation, by entering into sympathetic relations with the cosmos and discovering the correspondences between the macrocosm and the principles of man, the microcosm: this is cosmic consciousness, or 'macrocosmic consciousness.'

We must be careful to avoid the trap of thinking that the downward arc is evil and to be feared; it is the will of Almighty Zeus, father and creator, that his world should be filled with reason and beauty. It is the proceeding soul who moves in the mundane world and performs an essential duty. As Thomas Taylor says,[2] "the descent of intellect into the realms of generation becomes, indeed, the greatest benefit and ornament which a material nature is capable of receiving: for without the participation of intellect in the lowest regions of matter, nothing but irrational soul and a brutal life would subsist in its dark and fluctuating abode." And it is principally soul which provides the vehicle for the descent of intellect into the mundane.

The ascending arc of the circle is that of the greater mysteries, which are concerned, says Taylor in the same treatise,[3] with "the felicity of the soul both here and hereafter, when purified from the defilements of a material nature, and constantly elevated to the realities of intellectual vision." The ultimate goal of this arc is to arrive at the consciousness of the self (or 'microcosmic consciousness') and thence to rise to *henosis* or 'friendship with the Gods' - wherein the images of every God and Goddess are awakened from the depths of the soul, in which they were placed by the Demiurgus of the universe at the soul's creation. The arcs of the mysteries are shown in figure 7.

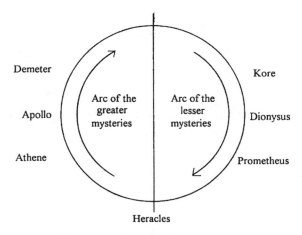

Figure 7: The arcs of the lesser and greater mysteries.

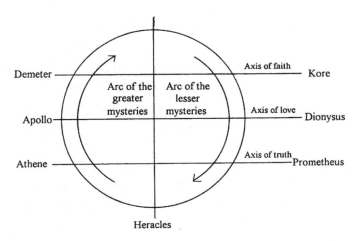

Figure 8: The initiations of the lesser and greater mysteries.

In the first arc the soul acts upon substances other than her own; in the second phase she acts entirely upon herself. In the first the aspiring mystic meditates upon the great ideas of the universe, while in second he or she contemplates the real being which lies hidden behind those great ideas.   There are correspondences between the stations of the two paths of initiation, which can be shown by combining the features of figures six and seven (pages 94 and 199) to produce our final diagram (figure 8).

In this diagram we see Heracles 'standing out', as it were, from the three divine axes. Is Heracles a man or a God? In the ancient world he was revered and worshipped as both.

In the *lesser* mysteries the initiation of *faith* is first: Kore has faith that Creation is joy-giving and beautiful, and she lays both hands upon the flower of Zeus – but she does not know the implications of her descent, and must, therefore, begin the cycle in faith.   Next follows the initiation of *love*, by which Dionysus impregnates the whole of Nature with beauty, scattering spirit into matter. Finally the soul undergoes the initiation of *truth*, for now the nature of the objective can be seen in relation to the hidden causes of the spiritual world – Promethean truth might be described as the correspondence of ideas to things. Once these three initiations have been experienced in lives and deaths, the soul, like Heracles, is ready for the ascent to Olympus. In the *greater* mysteries, the initiation of *truth* is first, for Athene guides the aspiring soul to see truth as the correspondence of thoughts to ideas, and by this means to pick out the invisible path to her true home.

Next comes the initiation of *love*, which is seen in the irresistible urge to the union, or the 'not-manyness' of Apollo. Lastly, the ultimate initiation is that of *faith*, as the soul makes her final surrender to the Great Mother Deeps: the finite being released into the infinite. What does the river know of the vast Ocean? Nothing, but –

> The river of green is sliding unseen beneath the trees,
> Laughing as it makes it way through the endless
> summer to the sea . . . .

Thus the cycle which was begun in the joy of the flower of the Father, is ended in the joy of the Mother.

The initiations of Faith, Love and Truth are explained by Proclus in his *Commentary on the First Alcibiades*:[4]

> There are, however, three monads according to these intelligible causes, subsisting uniformly and causally in intelligibles, but first unfolding themselves into light in the ineffable order of the Gods, I mean Faith, Truth, and Love. And Faith indeed establishes all things in good; but Truth unfolds all the knowledge in beings; and lastly, Love converts all things, and congregates them into the nature of the beautiful. This triad, indeed, thence proceeds through all the orders of the Gods, and imparts to all things, by its light, a union with intelligible itself. It also unfolds itself differently in different orders, every where combining its powers with the peculiarities of the Gods. And among some it subsists ineffably, incomprehensibly, and unifically; but among others, as the cause of connecting and binding; and among others, as endued with a perfective and forming power. Here again, it subsists intellectually and paternally; but

there in a manner entirely motive, vivific, and effective. Here, as governing and assimilating; there in a liberated and undefiled manner; and elsewhere according to a multiplied and dividing mode. Love, therefore, supernally descends from intelligibles to mundane natures, calling all things upwards to divine beauty. Truth also proceeds through all things, illuminating all things with knowledge. And lastly, Faith proceeds through the universe, establishing all things unically in good. Hence the Chaldæan oracles assert that all things are governed by, and abide in, these. *And on this account they order Theurgists to conjoin themselves to divinity through this triad.*

The initiations we undergo upon the universal circle are, properly speaking, interior and entirely unique to each individual: the map, it is said, is not the territory, and so what information is contained in the previous chapters will only be of use if the reader is made by it more sensitive to the inner experience. There is no teacher but the self, but the self can be alive with divinity: Divine Wisdom is 'given to all her children' and 'her delights are with the sons of men.'[5] In all the mythologies of the world the divinity of Wisdom is, even when also identified with war, presented as capable of great gentleness and love: it is Athene who begins the upward arc of the great mysteries and it is to Athene that Proclus addressed this hymn:[6]

> Great goddess, hear! and on my dark'ned mind
> Pour thy pure light in measure unconfin'd; -
> That sacred light, O all-protecting queen,
> Which beams eternal from thy face serene:

My soul, while wand'ring on the earth, inspire
With thy own blessed and impulsive fire;
And from thy fables, mystic and divine,
Give all her powers with holy light to shine.
Give love, give wisdom, and a power to love,
Incessant tending to the realms above . . . .

In the suggested interpretation of the myth of Athene we touched on the concept that to accomplish the Heracles task the soul must treat the mundane goal as all-important. There is a pivotal moment in the Bhagavad Gita in which the hero, Arjuna, is overlooking a battlefield upon which he is about to engage his enemy. The enemy army includes many of his relations and much-revered teachers, but these must be defeated if Arjuna is to obtain the kingdom which is rightfully his. In this myth-cycle the battle represents the Heraclean prize - in other words the external object of highest value; but Arjuna hesitates, and turning to Sri Krishna, the Divine Lord, who is acting as his charioteer, says that it would be better to live as a pauper than to kill these beloved relatives and friends. Here we see Arjuna turning from the viewpoint which values the external to the consideration which demands an internal ordering of self; in other words he is abandoning the arc of the lesser mysteries and seeking to begin the arc of the greater mysteries. What is the reaction of Krishna to this shift in goal? It is quite the opposite of what is normally considered the mystical counsel:[7]

Thou grievest for those who need no grief. The wise grieve neither for the living nor the dead. Verily, never was I not, nor thou, nor all of these,

nor ever shall we cease to be. As the dweller in
this body goes through childhood, youth, and aged
manhood, so he passeth on to other bodies. The
wise man grieveth not thereat. The contacts of
sense bring heat and cold, pleasure and pain; they
come and go, impermanent; bear with them as do
the wise.

Verily, the man who is not moved by these,
indifferent alike to sorrow and to joy, is meet for
immortality, O Chief of Men! The unreal hath no
being: the Real can never cease to be; to see the
truth of both, is theirs who reach the all-pervading
Essence. Know that That, by Whom the universe
is outspread, is imperishable. None can unmake the
works that the Eternal One doth make. Bodies
perish, but that One lives on, immutable and
endless.

He who deemeth That to be a slayer and he who
thinketh That is slain, both of these are
undiscerning. It slayeth not: neither is It slain. It
is never born: It never dieth. It never cometh into
being: It never ceaseth to be. Unborn, Undying,
Undiminishing, Primeval. This is not slain when
the body dieth. How can one, knowing This to be
Unborn, Undying, Imperishable, Ancient, cause any
to be slain, and whom can he slay?

As a man layeth aside outworn garments and
taketh others that are new, so the dweller in bodies
casteth off the old and entereth bodies that are new.
Weapons cleave not This; fire burneth It not;
waters wet not This, neither do winds dry It. This,
the Impenetrable, the Incombustible, the
Unmoistened, the Unparched; This, the Everlasting,
the All-pervasive, the Immutable, the Firm, the
Ancient of Days. This the Unmanifest is called,
Whom no thought can encompass; abiding ever in

Itself; therefore, knowing This thou shouldst not grieve. Or, if thou thinkest It is ever born and ever dies, even then thou shouldst not grieve. For the end of birth is death, and the end of death is birth: this is the Law, hence it is not meet for thee to mourn. The origin of beings is unperceived, so likewise is their end, but between these is that which is seen; what is there sorrowful in this? One may contemplate This as a marvel; another may tell of It as a marvel; another may hear of It as a marvel; but not one can thus the knowledge of This attain. This dweller in the body is invulnerable in every being; scorn thou to mourn, then, for that which cannot suffer.

Do thy part, be mindful of thy duty, and fear not, for to the warrior-guardian there is blessing in lawful strife. Happy is the martial soul who through such conquest findeth unsought the open door of Heaven. But if knowing thy duty and thy task, thou fail in their performance, then shall sin encompass thee. Thy dishonour will redound from age to age, and infamy is worse than death to him who loveth honour. It will seem that fear hath mastered thee, and thou wilt merit scorn from those who erstwhile honoured thee. Thou wilt suffer reproach for thy lack of strength, and what could befall thee more grievous than this? If slain, thou wilt obtain heaven: if victorious, thou wilt gain the fruits of earth; wherefore, arise, O Son, with firm resolve to conquer! Regard pleasure and pain, gain and loss, success and failure, all alike, but gird thyself for battle and thou shalt not suffer sin.

The path to the greater mysteries is through the successful accomplishment of the initiations of the lesser mysteries, then, and to attempt the latter without first completing the former is not the way of the soul. Now we are looking at the path of the soul as a simple linear one, with its distinct stations: this is only a convenient analysis for theoretical discussion, and in reality the soul lives all the stages all the time. We must "render unto Caesar what is Caesar's, and unto God what is God's" so that at one and the same time we turn downwards to implant the spirit in matter and turn upward to offer the first fruit -which is the self - to the heavenly Demeter. It is closer to the truth to say that our progress in the greater mysteries is dependent upon our successful continuance in the lesser mysteries.

We may say that the soul passes through the stages of the circle, but does not leave them behind: like those of a tree, the growth-rings of previous seasons are concealed within her depths. The seven stages are revealed in the seven principal characteristics of the soul:[8]

By the power of Kore, the soul is self-motive, and indivisible.

By the power of Dionysus, the soul is self-vital, and immortal.

By the power of Prometheus, the soul is self-subsistent, and indestructible.

By the power of Heracles, the soul is a form creator, and incorporeal.

By the power of Athene, the soul is a plural-unity, and perpetually active.

By the power of Apollo, the soul is a unity, and pure.

By the power of Demeter, the soul is a centre, and universal.

The mythological life is unavoidable, for each soul has set out on a path which demands a certain response. Our choice is whether to lead a conscious life of myth or an unconscious life of myth; in the latter suffering leads only to more suffering as the soul moves from dream to dream, but in the former, suffering leads to perfection and the union with one's leading God. The conscious life of myth is the life of the *telestai* or mystic who moves through the three stages - purification, initiation and interior inspection.

In the fullness of time we may be certain that all souls will return to the source, the 'river of souls' that is Demeter-Rhea, for the soul has as her very quintessence sacred reason; this is the guarantee of our salvation, which, after the operation of Heraclean virtue, leads us, divine step by divine step, to the ever-living Gods. As the Chaldean Oracles exhort:[9]

> Explore the river of the soul, whence, or in what order, having become a servant of the body, you may again rise to that order from which you flowed, uniting operation to sacred reason.

Notes

1. See pages 99-110, and especially p. 60; *Oracles and Mysteries*, The Prometheus Trust, 1995.

2. *Ibid.* p. 109.

3. *Ibid*, p. 78.

4. To be found in Proclus' *Theology of Plato*, VII, 41; The Prometheus Trust, Frome, 1996.

5. From Ecclesiasticus xxiv, 18 and Proverbs viii, 31.

6. See pages 251 to 252 of *Hymns and Initiations*, The Prometheus Trust, 1995.

7. *Bhagavad Gita*, II, 11 - 38, Shrine of Wisdom translation, Shrine of Wisdom, Godalming, 1927.

8. See the series of articles on 'The System of Plotinus' published in the Shrine of Wisdom Magazine between 1919 and 1921.

9. See page 8, *Oracles and Mysteries*, The Prometheus Trust, Frome, 1995.

Chapter Eleven

Plato's *Symposium*
and the
Seven Myths of the Soul

Urging thyself towards the centre of the sounding Light.
Apollo, subsisting as the principle of the choir of the Muses,
Which are around him, is a harmony of exulting light.
Chaldean Oracles CXLIV, CXLV.

Having explored the myth cycle outlined by Damascius,
using as our guide the philosophy of Plato and his
interpreters, it may be useful to change our perspective for
a chapter, and explore the philosophy of Plato using our
mythological perspective. To this end we will consider a
well-known dialogue, the *Symposium* (or *Banquet*), again
with due recognition that the limitations of a single
chapter for such a profound dialogue will entail some
simplifications and abridgments.

There are many ways to analyze Platonic dialogues -
logical, ethical, rational, theological and mystical, to name
but a few - some of which may have been in the mind of
Plato, and others not. The following scheme is mystical:
I think it likely that this outline, or something like it, was
indeed in Plato's thinking, although ultimately we cannot
know for certain. Whether or not this is so, I hope that
it provides some kind of framework for considering Plato's
Symposium mythologically.

Reasons for supposing the *Symposium* to be a mystical scheme

The whole dialogue is related by Apollodorus - literally "a gift of Apollo". Apollo stands in the scheme of inspiration (see the *Phædrus*) between the action of Dionysus which purifies the soul and renders it perfect as a dweller in objectivity or the 'projected universe' and that of Eros which enfolds the individual soul into the 'One and the All' (the final goal of Love). We will see references to the aphorisms of Apollo both at the beginning and the end of the dialogue.

The first aphorism we come across is 'nothing to excess' which was one of the three sayings which greeted pilgrims to the Sanctuary of Apollo at Delphi. Thus the decision to discourse on love is coupled with that of drinking only in moderation.

Diotima tells Socrates that he is being 'initiated and advanced' in the 'mysteries of love' (210a) There are other references to this to be found elsewhere in the reported speech of Diotima.

In the ancient mysteries of Ancient Greece the early stages were open to all who could understand Greek and who were unpolluted by murder: but the interior stages were secret, and only open to those who had been through the proper preparation. There was another notice at the entrance to the Sanctuary of Delphi: "Far off, ye profane, far off"; and at Eleusis, too, the uninitiated were driven out of the mystery site when the 'greater' mysteries were to be celebrated. Thus the words of Alcibiades, "But let the servants and any other profane and rustic person that may be present, close their ears with mighty gates" (218b), do not refer to the shame of a failed homosexual seduction but to the retelling of things which fall under the greater mysteries, and are a distinct reference to the Apollonic words.

There are other references to mystery celebrations in Alcibiades' speech, for example (216a) "For when I hear him [Socrates], my heart leaps much more than that of those who celebrate the mysteries of the Corybantes; and my tears flow from his discourse." The Corybantes are cathartic and defensive gods who are concerned, therefore, with the mysteries of Dionysus (*i.e.* those that are celebrated prior to the mysteries of Apollo). The tears refer to the tragic and comic dramas which formed the central element of the mystery celebrations and which are also referred to again at 233d.

The constant reference to drink and to the effects of drunkenness are, again, reminders of the orgies of Dionysus, who is the God of wine as well as of separation. Socrates' immunity to the effects of alcohol, mentioned by Alcibiades and remarked upon by Apollodorus at the end, is an indication that Socrates is under the influence of Apollo and not Dionysus; for Apollo, as we have seen, unifies and harmonises, while Dionysus separates and causes argument - as any witness to closing time in the public house will concede!

The speeches of the *Banquet* and the seven myths of the soul

There are seven main speakers at Plato's *Symposium*, as retold by Apollodorus; we will look at each in turn in the light of both the seven myths and Campbell's scheme of the hero's journey.

The symposium at which the speeches were made followed a more wine-soaked revel of the previous night, and so the participants had agreed to moderate their drinking and, in the place of their normal pleasures, make speeches in praise of Love.

1 'The call to adventure', Kore, and the speech of Phædrus

It falls to Phædrus to make the opening speech, since it was originally his idea that Love should be praised in this manner. Phædrus claims that Love was among the first of Gods - referring to the Theogony *of Hesiod - and that he had no parents; on this account, Phædrus says, "Love was powerful, and wonderfully great, both on Earth and among the Gods." To young persons there is no greater good, for Love and the desire to be well thought of by one's lover drives the young to the finest and noblest of deeds, even, ultimately, to sacrifice their own lives if the circumstances arise.*

In this speech we see all the hall-marks of Persephone: it is, of all seven speeches, the most naive, since there is no attempt to analyze love; Phædrus, it seems, is overwhelmed by the power of Love - in fact he says that Love is a "force resistless" (179b). We do not have to look too hard at this to see the simplicity of the virgin Persephone, who is overwhelmed by her husband-to-be. The whole of the last half of the speech is concerned with the idea of dying for love, which is exactly the experience of Kore, who dies to the world of her Divine Mother when the desire of Hades sweeps her downwards into his kingdom. Our soul, too, as we have seen in previous chapters, dies to the world of spirit when we plunge into objectivity. The first half of the speech having established Love as the earliest of Gods, centres on the power of Love in the young, "at their first setting out in life" (178b) which is, of course, the position of Persephone as representing the 'call to adventure.' Phædrus, who as the originator of the symposium, has most clearly heard the 'call to adventure' and such is the power of his inspiration, he takes all the other participants upon the adventure of praising Love. Love, he says, leads the young out into the world because "consanguinity has not the power to excite us" as much as Love (178c); we, when we are young, make the object of our love some external mistress. And this is, of course, the nature of material manifestation, which has little consanguinity to the soul; the call of Love is the call to adventure in strange lands, and having heard and responded to it, the soul *must* perform her heroic deeds before eventually arriving at the "islands of the blest." (180b)

2 'The crossing of the threshold', Dionysus, and the speech of Pausanias

Following the simple speech of Phædrus, Pausanias starts his speech with the first analysis of the dialogue: he divides Love into vulgar and celestial Love, again referring to mythological stories as well as common experience. The lower form of love is held to be degrading and Pausanias says that those in the grip of such a love "choose from the object of their passion the silliest creatures they can light on: for, confining their views to the gratification of their passion by the act of enjoyment, they are regardless in what manner they gratify it . . ." But, he says, the higher forms of Love do bring great benefits, one of which is the tendency of the lovers of this kind to oppose tyranny. Such is the great esteem in which love of this kind is held, those activities which would normally be censured - making vows and oaths, keeping nightly vigils, voluntarily stooping to such slavery as no slave would undergo - are considered admirable between lovers; even lying, if one is under the influence of Love, is permissible. All in all, while the actions undertaken for the sake of vulgar love are rarely desirable, almost anything is permitted to the celestial lover.

The end of this speech brings a drunken attack of hiccups to Aristophanes, so that he is unable to take his proper turn after Pausanias.

It is Pausanias who first puts forward the idea that love is twofold: the celestial and the 'vulgar' Venus (180d). This is the very essence of crossing the threshold in Campbell's analysis, for the overwhelming impression of the hero as he moves into a new realm of experience is that of the twoness of things - including himself. We will see that this twoness remains a constant theme amongst the speakers, becoming more and more pronounced until Socrates heals the division. Campbell himself notes that as the hero sets off in mythological stories he very often meets 'the goddess' or 'the temptress' - in Pausanias' terms, the celestial and the vulgar Venuses. The myth of Dionysus carries with it this division as its central theme, and implicit within the activities of Dionysus is the idea of breaking up the *status quo* - either through degeneration or through the overwhelming of one set of laws by a higher: Pausanias says that of those activities normally condemned in ordinary life "in a lover all this is graceful" (183b). We have seen from our examination of the myth of Dionysus how the coming of the God was viewed with great anxiety by those in authority, for this very reason.

A more fitting end to a speech undertaken under the governance of Dionysus - that of a listener becoming unable to speak because of drunken hiccups - is difficult to imagine.

3 'Trials', Prometheus, and the speech of Eryximachus

Eryximachus agrees with the previous speaker, that there are two Loves, because there are two Aphrodites. This speaker is a physician and immediately introduces the idea of the differences between the diseased and healthy body, suggesting that the love of the diseased is like the lower love, but the love of the healthy body, like the higher love. The physician, he

*says, must attempt to reconcile opposites - cold and hot, bitter
and sweet, dry and moist, and so on - and this is the very
action of love. The reconciling and harmonising power of the
higher love brings many benefits, while the same power of the
lower love brings the ruin and corruption of natures with
"diseases . . . mildews, hail-storms, and blights." Even our
relations to the Gods is retarded by the wrong kind of love,
as we fall into injustice, but the same relations are
characterised by justice and piety when regulated by the higher
love. The power of both kinds of love extend from the highest
human relations to the Gods, right down through the different
levels of lives, as far at least as to animal and vegetative life.*

Although the crossing of the threshold produces the
sensation of twoness, it is the tasks and tests which must
be accomplished in the otherworld which enable the hero
to understand the different qualities of each of the two
principles (self and not-self, spirit and matter, consciousness
and sub- or super-consciousness, etc). It is the attempt at
the tests which is the all-important thing here, not their
successful conclusion: often, it seems, the hero will fail in
his tests but somehow carry on. Eryximachus, being a
physician, is especially concerned with the trials which
beset the soul in its mundane life: much of the speech
concerns the harmonizing of the two sides of mortal
nature. Undoubtedly Eryximachus is more aware than
Pausanias of the duality of human life and human love: this
is because he is undergoing the trials of the dual life - the
awareness of twoness of the 'crossing of the threshold'
becoming a harsh actuality in the 'trial' phase. The myth
of Prometheus being bound to the rocks of the Caucasian

mountains with an eagle or vulture devouring his liver by day (it grew back again at night) stands for these trials which, so often, seem never-ending and almost unendurable. Eryximachus defines the action of desires as that "filling and emptying" (186c), which precisely matches the torment of Prometheus. The desires which underscore the activities of plant, animal and human life are the instinctive desires that truly bind the soul to body. Porphyry, in his *Auxiliaries to Perception of the Intelligible*,[1] says that nature binds body to the soul but that the soul binds herself to the body: the first bonds are released by the natural processes of death, but the bonds which the soul makes are only released by the soul's powers: the ordination or otherwise of the instinctive nature is the subject of the true physician, and the trials and chains of Prometheus.

4 'Sacred marriage/apotheosis', Heracles, and the speech of Aristophanes

Aristophanes, once he is able to speak after his attack of hiccups, begins by suggesting that man is actually a halved creature, having once been eight-limbed and double-headed, but having been punished for an attempt to storm heaven by being split into two incomplete beings as we now know ourselves. This is, he says, the reason why both love and sex have such a power over humans - for we are pursuing, quite literally, our other halves, in order to re-unite ourselves. Since some of the original eight-limbed creatures were male, others female, and yet others hermaphrodite, Aristophanes says that some pursue their search in those of same sex, and others in the opposite sex: he further claims that those who were originally male were the best, so that those who seek their other half in their fellow males are of the best disposition. Love, he says, is our greatest comfort in our present situation, and will lead us, if we pay due regard and reverence to the Gods, to the recovery of our ancient, whole nature, making us blest and happy.

Campbell calls this phase 'sacred marriage,' 'atonement' or 'apotheosis' and we can see each of these ideas emerging in Aristophanes' speech. We can see, too, that this speech marks the furthest extent of the consciousness of division - man in his present state is actually only a half of himself - as well as indicating the need for enduring the evils of our divided existence (193d). Since this speech corresponds to the myth of Heracles we should not be surprised if the maker of it praises the all-male 'halves' above the other two combinations, nor that Aristophanes names Hephaistos as the God who might join the two halves together again, for Hephaistos is the God who is concerned with *mundane* fabrication and Heracles is the conqueror of the mundane world. There is some disagreement amongst modern commentators as to whether Plato gives to Aristophanes the most coherent and substantial speech after Socrates or whether he gives him the most superficial and least worthy one: this ambiguity is indicative of the position of Heracles who is both the finest exponent of human achievement and at the same time, the most distant from the Platonic ideal of spiritual realisation. The name

Aristophanes, by the way, means 'bringing the best to light', which is another way of looking at the position of Heracles who makes manifest the inherent *arete*, or excellences of the soul.

5 'Flight', Athene, and the speech of Agatho

Agatho begins his speech by claiming that, firstly, Love is the most youthful of the Gods, since he flees and outruns old age; secondly, that Love was not the ruler of the heavens in the earliest tales of the Gods, but Necessity; and thirdly, that Love is tender and yielding, so that he easily penetrates our inmost soul. Furthermore, he says, Love is greater in valour than Mars, as Love is able to master all, and all who are inspired by Love become masters of their chosen activity. Love, Agatho claims, enables men to rise from disorder and savagery to the best conditions and should, therefore, be followed by all. Love is portrayed as the highest God, "blest above all others," and is greatest in beauty and goodness.

Agatho's speech with its references to the fleet-footed God of Love who outruns Old Age (195b) establishes the image of 'flight' at its outset. Although Agatho is aware of duality within and without the human soul his view of Love is that it "overlooks evil" and "observes the good" (197d). Love's power over Ares, the war-god, reminds us of Athene's greater power of battle mentioned in chapter seven. All virtues are at the command of the true lover (196b) - wisdom, temperance, justice and fortitude - so that the summation of the Heraclean tasks is found in the next step of the sevenfold path under the rulership of Athene. Agatho claims that Necessity has been the ruler on the downward arc previous to this point, but that from hereon Love becomes the ruler of a benevolent and good society. The flight, then, is from the inflexible rule of Necessity (in incarnation) towards the golden realm of Love (in spirit); the myths prior to those of Athene do indeed involve a degree of compulsion, and Kore, Dionysus and Prometheus can be seen as suffering victims, and even Heracles is under an obligation to Eurystheus in his most important myth. On the other hand, Athene, Apollo and Demeter are much more clearly free agents in their myths. The soul under the aegis of Athene is the civilising and artistic builder (197b), bringing order out of disorder and the 'good society' out of savagery. Agatho explicitly mentions, among other social activities, the order of dance (197d), from which the name Pallas is derived.

6 'Return', Apollo, and the speech of Socrates

Between Agatho's speech and that of Socrates there is a short dialogue between the two; in it Socrates challenges Agatho's assertion of Love's pre-eminence. Love, says Socrates, is the desire of something, and the desire of something indicates a lack of that thing; and since Love at its best is the love of Beauty, Love is through this syllogistic reasoning proved to be lacking beauty, and since beauty is goodness made manifest, he is also lacking the good. To explain the implications of this, Socrates repeats the teaching he received from the priestess

Diotima, which had started when Socrates had made similar assertions to those of Agatho. Love, said Diotima, being the offspring of Poverty and Plenty, actually possesses a middle characteristic; he feels intense lack but has great abilities to pursue that which he lacks. In truth, she continued, Love is a great dæmon - that is a mediator between men and Gods - through whom we are properly able to aspire to the Good and the Beautiful. The domain of Love is universal, since beings desire both the Good and the Beautiful, and, therefore, all activities of every creature created by the Gods can be seen in terms of the power of love. Man himself starts with the lower levels of consciousness and aspiration (that of separated bodies) and rises to the very highest level (that of the One Beauty) by following the path of love. Seeking union with eternal beauty, man reaches the point at which he generates true virtue, and then, if ever any man may, she says, he lives the immortal life.

It is interesting to note that Damascius draws Athene and Apollo together as those who aid the soul to 'collect herself'; the only substantial mixing of speakers in the *Symposium* reflects this, as the dialogue between Agatho and Socrates mixes their different positions on Love into one (199d ff). The return, or the 'recrossing of the threshold' is the point at which the hero returns to his previous emplacement; but while the emplacement is superficially the same in truth, because the hero has undergone his various experiences, his condition within that emplacement is not the same. The ignorance of duality which he had in the first stage (the 'call to adventure') has been removed, while the memory of unity which had been lost in the ensuing stages is recovered. The hero is now able, by his own powers, to reconcile the above and below, the abstract and material, the self and not-self, unity and multiplicity. Thus it is that Socrates, with the interior teaching of Diotima made his own, is able to see the whole range of love not as separated levels - celestial and vulgar, or body, ethics, art, science, etc. - but as a continuum. Even the lowest levels of love are, says Diotima, expressions of the entire universe's desire of the One Good (or the Eternal Beauty) and to possess this Good in perpetuity (207a-d). Of course, the highest praise is reserved for the One Beauty which is the cause of all other beauties, for in the permanent union with this source we become, if any mortal can, like a God (212b). If Athene reconciles opposites, Apollo truly unifies the parts into one whole: it is clear that Socrates is, in Plato's *Symposium*, an Apollonic hero. The loving use of dialectic to remove the separating influence of false concepts is Socrates' equivalent of Apollo's golden sword. The return to the spiritual realm cannot be accomplished until the soul has realized her unity: it is Apollo, the 'not many' who effects this realization. It is entirely appropriate that the voice of Apollo is first expressed by a priestess (in this case Diotima), and then explained by a wise interpreter (Socrates) - for this was exactly the pattern established in the announcement of the oracles at the Delphic Sanctuary of Apollo.

7 'Elixir', Demeter, and the speech of Alcibiades

*After Socrates has finished speaking, Aristophanes attempts
to speak in reply but is interrupted by loud knocking from the
door to the outside: this signals the arrival of a drunken
Alcibiades, who, having heard of the nature of the preceding
speeches, demands his turn. He begins his speech with a
complaint - that Socrates, no matter how much he drinks, will
not become drunk - and then compares him with Silenuses;
these are statues of flute players which can be opened to reveal
smaller statues of Gods within. In fact, says Alcibiades,
outwardly Socrates resembles Marsyas but when he speaks he
moves the heart more that the 'mysteries of the Corybantes.'
He then relates an attempt he made to seduce Socrates by
lying beside him after a late evening of discourse: the attempt
failed, Socrates bidding Alcibiades to pursue inner rather than
outer beauty. Socrates, he says, seems to deceive many young
men who think that he wishes to be their lover, but in fact
only wishes to enlighten them with numerous images of
virtue.*

It might seem that the sixth speech is the end of the
serious business of the *Symposium*, and that the
enlightenment which is Socrates' is the final initiation. But
this is not so: the whole weary journey would be a
nonsense if the hero-soul were merely to return to her
pristine condition full of wisdom but doing nothing with
it. The soul may be seen as 'creativity-in-action' and the
fully realized soul can now be seen as a co-ruler with the
Demiurge. The returned hero, bringing the elixir, is now
able to help others to attain to the same condition as

himself. Thus Alcibiades is actually describing Socrates not as an enlightened man, but as a returned hero who, with the aid of his discourses, moves amongst the Athenians drawing out the wisdom inherent in others. The entire tone of Alcibiades' speech is one of hero-worship: and this is because Socrates stands as Plato's perfected-man, his Buddha, his Christed mortal; his returned hero. Socrates speaking represents Apollo, for here he acts as a herdsmen of his auditors; but Socrates as a living model represents Demeter, as a seed of spiritual enlightenment buried deep in the heart of the aspiring individual.

Demeter, as the Goddess of harvest and fruit, is especially connected to that completion which hands on to the coming generation all that is good and nourishing: the hero under Demeter is no longer serving his own perfection but the universe's perfection; he operates not, as in the Herculean stage of mundane conquest, as a soul in the processes of time and space, but 'essentially' or operating without process, from his very being. (Note that Aristophanes' - the dialogue's Heracles - attempt to speak after Socrates to this point fails, 212c.) The archetype of man is held within the Divine Mother as an eternal principle: it is not the being of man but rather the cause of his being. The great mystical religions of the world each have their own way of expressing this inexpressible principle: the Vedas, for example, say it is 'the self, deep-seated in the heart, Atman, all-self of selves'. Demeter, as goddess of seed, rules over the infinite-infinitesimal point within the deeps of each mortal and immortal. Plato's image of the Silenuses (215b) is, of course, a perfect representation of a seed, since the truly productive part of the fruit is always contained in a husk or outer skin. Further, he compares Socrates' appearance to Marsyas (215b), the very piper whom Apollo flayed alive (that is, removed the outer covering) when he failed to match the God's music. Alcibiades' attempted seduction of Socrates was the beautiful young man's attempt to get Socrates to move towards himself; but Socrates' response was the true image of one who has 'died to the body' and understands that the greatest love is that of the Gods, who[2] 'lead and perfect all things by their very being.' Alcibiades' constant references to the mysteries (for example at 215d) with regard to his experience of Socrates is an indication that the Demeter state of 'elixir' has been reached: once, he says (217a), he had seen the true nature of the inner Socrates he considered it "so divine, golden, all-beautiful and wonderful, that I was determined to act in every respect conformably to the advice of Socrates." The golden-haired Demeter was the founder and focus of the greatest mysteries of Greece, the most advanced of which entailed the gates of the sanctuary at Eleusis being closed to those who were not yet ready for the final initiation - a fact recalled by Alcibiades' words as he is about to reveal the true measure of Socrates' rulership of himself (218b): "But let the servants, or any other profane and rustic person that may be present, close their ears with mighty gates."

The philosophical friends gathered around the table are inspired by the "Bacchic fury of philosophy" (218b), which starts, I suggest, with the original 'crossing of the threshold' and ends with the 'return' or 'recrossing of the threshold' - in other words embraced by souls in the lower half of the circle - but Socrates, as a model of divinized man, is once again in the upper half of the circle, beyond the reach of the intoxication of wine, the juice of Bacchus. The dialogue ends with Socrates walking away from the party completely unaffected by the night's drinking.

Notes

1. Porphyry's *Auxiliaries to the Perception the Intelligible*, section viii, TTS vol. II, p. 170.

2. Proclus *Theology of Plato*, I, xiv, TTS vol. VIII, p. 94.

Chapter Twelve

A defence of the worship of the Gods

For a good man to sacrifice to and be conversant with
the GODS, is of all things the most beautiful, the best,
and the most useful to the possession of a happy life.
Plato's Laws V

We have now completed our survey of the seven myths
of Damascius, and considered both the soul and divinity in
their light. A final diversion from the main theme of this
book is, however, required here if we are to remain
faithful to the doctrines of Plato.

In the second and third books of the *Republic* (377a
onwards), Plato famously exiles Homer and mythologising
poets generally from his ideal city. This is a thoroughly
misunderstood passage, and one that needs careful
examination, if we are not to reject an invaluable part of
mankind's tradition.

The dismissal of Homer is prompted by the suggestion
that myths of a poetical kind - as opposed the philosophic
myths with which Plato adorns his writings - may lead to
gross errors in the thinking of the Republic's citizens.
Over the centuries, and especially in our own time, this
has been taken to mean that Plato rejected poetry as well
as fantastical myth. Is this true? Not so, I think, unless
we are to accuse Plato of the most ridiculous hypocrisy,
for the divine philosopher hardly allows a single dialogue

to pass without a direct or indirect reference to the words of Homer. In the *Laws*, for example there are five direct quotes from the poet, all spoken with approval.[1] If Plato cannot exile Homer from his own writings, he can hardly have expected him to have been barred from his city.

Plato's concern about these poetical myths, to be precise, is that they are liable to introduce to the minds of the young citizens, misconceptions about the Gods. A great deal of the *Republic* is about the way in which the state should go about educating its young, and, having paid so much attention to this vital area, Plato does not want the whole enterprise undermined by such misconceptions. To Plato the most important dogma concerning the Gods is that they are entirely good, being the fountain-heads, as it were, of Providence. To suggest, in the light of this dogma, that Kronos ate his children, that Zeus was a serial adulterer, that the Olympians spent much of their time squabbling, that they can be bribed with a few sacrifices, and that the Goddess-inspired heroes of the great myths committed gross immoralities, would confound and confuse. The educators of the Republic would use only those myths which upheld the essential doctrines concerning the Gods when cultivating the minds of the young.

But, of course, within the state which is being planned there is an inner education for those whose abilities and perseverance have proved them to be worthy of further study. This deeper education would, one assumes, be very similar to that which Plato was promulgating within his academy: *this* education clearly used the poetic myth, as

Plato's own writing confirms and as he explicitly states in the *Laws*,[2] where the Guest says "But perhaps we old men should hear with the most pleasure the rhapsodist when properly handling the *Iliad* and *Odyssey*, or some of the works of Hesiod, and should by far proclaim him the victor of all the others." The other institution which, from Plato's perspective, legitimately unfolded the ancient myths was the mystery cults, since Plato writes in the most positive terms of the mystery sanctuaries and their work, for example in the *Phædrus*. In this dialogue Socrates tells Phædrus that the beauty of the divine heavens has been glimpsed by each soul as she joined the procession of the Gods to feast (every soul following her own particular Divinity), and that it is the reminiscence of this beauty which prompts us to make the difficult journey back to the spiritual realms. He says:[3]

> And we indeed beheld the Beautiful together with Jupiter, but others in conjunction with some other God; at the same time being initiate in those mysteries which it is lawful to call the most blessed of all mysteries.

By which, says Proclus, Plato means the Eleusinian mysteries. These mysteries undoubtedly used the myth of Demeter and Persephone as their central device for unfolding the true nature of the immortal soul. Earlier in the dialogue,[4] too, Socrates had praised the inspired priestesses, prophetesses, and sibyls who presided over the sanctuaries at such places at Dodona and Delphi - centres solemnised by their place in myth. If further proof is needed of Plato's endorsement of the mysteries, perhaps Socrates' words in the *Phædo* might be worth quoting:

> And those who instituted the mysteries for us appear to have been by no means contemptible persons, but to have really signified formerly, in an obscure manner, *that whoever descended into Hades uninitiated, and without being a partaker of the mysteries, should be plunged into mire; but that whoever arrived there, purified and initiated, should dwell with the Gods.* For, as it is said by those who write about the mysteries,
>
>> The thyrsus-bearers numerous are seen,
>> But few the Bacchuses have always been.

Our exploration of the myths concerning Dionysus and Prometheus are sufficient, I think, to determine what Plato says here is directly related to them.

The myths, then, which we have considered in this book, are the myths suitable for those who have a good philosophic background, and those who are willing to accept the discipline of the mysteries.

Now I have no reason to doubt the intelligence or the piety of those readers who have reached these closing chapters: however, I do think it worthwhile to unfold the philosophical truths without which one's understanding of the Gods may, like the youth from whom Homer is to be kept in Plato's *Republic*, become clouded. I think it unlikely that precisely the same confusion will be a problem with the modern reader as was the case with the ancient hearer of myths; the misconception which worried Plato when he looked at the conceptions of his non-philosophic contemporaries was that of literalism, which gives rise to superstition. Plato touches on this theme in the *Euthyphro*[5] when Socrates (who is about to be tried by the Athenians) inquires of Euthyphro why this young man is persecuting his father in a court of law? The reply being

-

> For men are firmly persuaded that Jupiter is the best and most just of gods, and yet they acknowledge that he put his father in chains, because he unjustly swallowed his children; and again, that Saturn castrated his father, through other things of a similar nature: but they are indignant with me, because I prosecute my father who has acted unjustly; and thus these men assert things contrary to each other in what they say concerning the gods and concerning me.
>
> SOC. Is this the thing then, Euthyphro, on account of which I am brought to the bar, because when any one asserts things of this kind concerning the gods, I admit them with pain; and through which, as it seems, some one calls me an offender? Now, therefore, if these things thus appear also to you who are well acquainted with such particulars, it is necessary, as it seems, that we also should admit them. For what else can we say, who acknowledge that we know nothing about such things? But tell me, by Jupiter, who presides over friendship; *do you think that these things thus happened in reality?*
>
> EUTH. Yes, and things still more wonderful than these, Socrates, of which the multitude are ignorant.
>
> SOC. Do you therefore think that the gods *in reality* wage war with each other, and that there are among them dire enmities and battles, and many other such like particulars as are related by the poets, with the representation of which by good

painters our temples are decorated; and in the great
Panathenææ a veil full of such like variegated
ornaments is carried into the Acropolis. Must we
say, O Euthyphro, that these things are true?

EUTH. Not these only, O Socrates; but, as I just
now said, I can relate to you many other things
concerning divine affairs if you are willing, which
when you hear I well know that you will be
astonished.

To which Socrates replies with his accustomed irony, "I
should not wonder!" In his own trial, Socrates, who is
accused of not believing in the ancient Gods of Greece,
tells his prosecutors "*I believe that there are* GODS *more
than any one of my accusers;*" - but it is clear that he is
anxious that men should understand that these Gods and
Goddesses are above the mythological stories told about
them.

The misconception many hold today, and which can be
reinforced by the study of myths, is that the Gods are
constructions of human ingenuity, or the unconscious
impulses of the psyche, or, at best, they are the brilliant
projections of man's deepest knowledge. The stories of
mythological battles, loves, heroics and treacheries are
obviously, exactly of this nature. But we must be clear as
to the nature of the reality in which these myths arise.
Simply put, the modern may claim that there is a spiritual
core in man which produces, simultaneously, myths and
Gods, and that these constructs, because they are from his
own depths, are endlessly fascinating to the enquiring
consciousness of man. But in reality, at least as far as
Platonism would have it, the Gods produce the spiritual

depth (as well as the miraculous cosmos), which in turn produces images of the Gods in myth. We can summarize the Platonic theological cosmology in one simple phrase: *The Gods are, and so the universe arises.* The Universe has being because there are Gods of Being; it has life because there are Gods of Life; it has intellect because there are Gods of Intellect; within it there are souls because there are Gods of Soul; within it there is nature because there are Gods of Nature; and there are bodies because there are Mundane Gods.

The pure teaching concerning the Gods, according to such great men as Proclus, Damascius and Syrianus, is that they are above sense, imagination, reason, intuition and every other species of knowledge and science at man's disposal. In truth we can know nothing of the Gods themselves since they all largely partake of the simple transcendency of The One. The highest mystical states, according to the ancient teachers, are those in which every finite reality (or, alternatively, illusion) is dismissed, and the soul enters the shining void, the true reality of which the tongue cannot speak, nor hand write.

But if we can know nothing of the Gods themselves, paradoxically, we know nothing which is not from the Gods. How can this be? Perhaps it is best to remember that our eyes cannot look directly at the sun, unless it is dimmed by the cloudy atmosphere of the earth, and yet our eyes are entirely dependent upon the light which the sun generates. In the same manner we cannot know (at least in our condition as a finite beings) the purest unity of beauty but every beauty we come to know either sensibly or rationally tells us something of that One Beauty.

But now we find ourselves at a seemingly impossible barrier, for no matter how many aspects of beauty (or anything else) we understand, still we cannot truly know the infinite Beauty: this Beauty is unific and simple, and the beauties of multiplicity, in the final analysis, obscure our vision of its oneness. Our task, then, is not to pursue external beauties (except insofar as they prompt us to turn to the beauty within ourselves) but to find some way of discovering our spiritual identity - and thus move our sensitivities, our consciousness and, indeed, our whole selves into the infinite. Platonists describe this as 'the alone calling to the alone', and Plotinus[6] puts it thus: "Every one, therefore, must become divine, and of godlike beauty, before he can gaze upon a god, and the beautiful itself."

How are we to 'become divine'? One of the ways that wise men and women throughout the ages have attempted this is through divine worship by which the worshippers become more and more attuned to the God or Goddess worshipped: this is perhaps best understood by the analogy of the sympathetic strings of instruments such as the sitar. The sitar has a small number of strings which are plucked, and a much greater number which are never plucked but which vibrate 'in sympathy' with the plucked strings. Each sympathetic string will only vibrate, however, if it is tuned to one of the notes of the plucked string. It is a question, then, of tuning ourselves to the *Henads* or Divine Unities by communion with them: the communion can be by prayer, hymn, meditation, contemplation, sacrifice or other ritual actions.

Of prayer, Iamblichus writes:[7]

> As prayers, through which sacred rites receive their perfect consummation and vigour, constitute a great part of sacrifice, and as they are of general utility to religion, and produce an indissoluble communion between the Divinities and their priests, it is necessary that we should mention a few things concerning their various species and wonderful effects. For prayer is of itself a thing worthy to be known, and gives greater perfection to the science concerning the Gods. I say, therefore, that the *first* species of prayer is *collective,* producing a contact with Divinity, and subsisting as the leader and light of knowledge. But the *second* is the *bond of consent and communion with the Gods,* exciting them to a copious communication of their benefits prior to the energy of speech, and perfecting the whole of our operations previous to our intellectual conceptions. But the *third* and most perfect species of prayer is *the seal of ineffable union with the Divinities,* in whom it establishes all the power and authority of prayer: and thus causes the soul to repose in the Gods, as in a divine and never-failing port. But from these three terms, in which all the divine measures are contained, suppliant adoration not only conciliates to us the friendship of the Gods, but supernally extends to us three fruits, being, as it were, three Hesperian apples of gold. The *first* pertains to *illumination;* the second, to *a communion of operation;* but through the energy of the *third* we receive *a perfect plenitude of divine fire.*

The philosopher must champion the cause of intellect, in its highest term, but Proclus, in his Commentary on the *Parmenides* (which incidentally he subtitles 'On the Gods'), warns that such is the progress of the thinker as he ascends the ladder of true dialectic by removing from apparent reality all spurious accretions, that he may arrive at a kind of nothingness: he, so to speak, who attempts to find the One, finds Nothing. His words are:[8]

> But our intention in pursuing these mysteries is no other than by the logical energies of our reason to arrive at the simple intellection of beings, and by these to excite the divine one resident in the depths of our essence, or rather which presides over our essence, that we may perceive the simple and incomprehensible one. For after, through discursive energies and intellections, we have properly denied of the first principle all conditions peculiar to beings, there will be some danger, lest, deceived by imagination after numerous negations, we should think that we have arrived either at nothing, or at something slender and vain, indeterminate, formless, and confused; unless we are careful in proportion as we advance in negations to excite by a certain amatorial affection the divine vigour of our unity; trusting that by this means we may enjoy divine unity, when we have dismissed the motion of reason and the multiplicity of intelligence, and tend through unity alone to *The One Itself,* and through love to *the supreme and ineffable good.*

The worship of the Gods, then, is the means by which the amatory impulse of the human soul is strengthened and purified, so that the final ascent to *The One* can be made.

This was the basis of the ancient world-view of religion, that in the great army of Gods there dwells the ineffable spirit of *The One* and that therefore no rivalry exists between them, despite appearances to the contrary in myths. It is, of course, an irony of no small degree that the orthodox monotheistic understanding of polytheism is that it is a system of warring rivalries, but that instances of human wars based on religious differences in the polytheistic Mediterranean world are scarcely to be found, while the catalogue of wars between the different worshippers of the so-called one god is long, bitter, bloody and tear-stained.

It is the life of loving prayer of the Gods which allows the philosopher-mystic the final power which is to arrive at the *adytum*, the inner recess of the temple, of the One and the Good. I can do no better than to quote one of the loveliest ever passages of any scripture:[9]

> Let us now therefore, if ever, abandon multiform knowledge, exterminate from ourselves all the variety of life, and in perfect quiet approach near to the cause of all things. For this purpose, let not only opinion and phantasy be at rest, nor the passions alone which impede our anagogic impulse to the first, be at peace; but let the air be still, and the universe itself be still. And let all things extend us with a tranquil power to communion with the ineffable. Let us also, standing there, having transcended the intelligible (if we contain any thing of this kind,) and with nearly closed eyes adoring as it were the rising sun, since it is not lawful for any being whatever intently to behold him - let us survey the sun whence the light of the

intelligible Gods proceeds, emerging, as the poets say, from the bosom of the ocean; and again from this divine tranquillity descending into intellect, and from intellect, employing the reasonings of the soul, let us relate to ourselves what the natures are from which, in this progression, we shall consider the first God as exempt. And let us as it were celebrate him, not as establishing the earth and the heavens, nor as giving subsistence to souls, and the generations of all animals; for he produced these indeed, but among the last of things; but, prior to these, let us celebrate him as unfolding into light the whole intelligible and intellectual genus of Gods, together with all the supermundane and mundane divinities - as the God of all Gods, the unity of all unities, and beyond the first adyta, - as more ineffable than all silence, and more unknown than all essence, - as holy among the holies, *and concealed in the intelligible Gods.*

Divine worship, it seems, is identical with the highest contemplation, which merges soundlessly into union. But, one might ask, why worship the Gods, rather than a direct worship of The One, who, after all, is the final object of every being? The answer is simple: *the One as the One is not approachable except through the Gods*, in just the same way as the sun is not perceivable except by the eyes that look upon its many rays. Religions which try to remove Gods from the scheme of worship nearly always unwittingly degrade God, or elevate man to a false and arrogant status. Very often God is seen primarily as the Creator; but the theology of Plato, and the great prophets of antiquity, show that the act of Creation is the least act of Divinity - as Proclus implies in the above passage.

Monotheism has at its centre a most precious truth - but to deny the Gods is to deny to The One the highest and most beautiful of powers, which is to unfold the Gods without diminishing in power, in reality, or in goodness. I must repeat the words of Proclus: *The One* is concealed in the intelligible Gods - who are the highest order of Gods, dwelling on the very threshold of the first God.

Furthermore, as much as some try to avoid it, monotheism always tends to diminish the importance of the Cosmos, which, without the ever-living Gods taking their place as rulers of it as well as within it, becomes a merely passive receptacle of divine and human power. Plato says over and over again, that *the world is a God*.[10] I will not labour this point, but urge the reader to look at what a culture which is basically a monotheistic one has done to that portion of the Cosmos over which it has influence.

Worship is the imitation and communion with that which is worshipped: it entails the worshipper following the essential characteristic of the God worshipped. But the essential characteristic of The One is transcendent unity, which, therefore, requires the devotee to cast away all that is not concerned with this 'oneness of oneness.' This is dependent upon the worshipper finding within himself or herself that which is only one, so that the "alone can fly to the alone." But this oneness of the self is the most difficult of all things to find, since it is almost nothing and is hidden by all the other principles of man; no man or woman will know his or her own oneness without first knowing him- or her-self, and all the great realities of the scheme of things which is the unfoldment of The One into manifestation. The attempt to cast away that which is not of the simple transcendent unity before this unity is properly identified will be unsuccessful and, furthermore, *will cause the devotee to dishonour and despise those very things in which the unity is hidden.* The greatest human evils arise when a great idea is applied raw, so to speak, at too low a level - when mystical truths are taken without careful adaptation into everyday life.

The worship of the Gods affirms the reality and honour of that which each God unfolds into light: to worship Zeus, the father and maker of the projected world, is to affirm in the highest degree the worth of his Cosmos, or beautiful order; to worship Athene is to affirm and honour the saving wisdom of divinity; to worship Demeter-Rhea is to affirm and honour the life which pervades every atom and cell, every animal and soul in the Cosmos. If these things are to be laid aside for the sake of the soul's ultimate worship of The One, they must be affirmed, honoured, and known for what they truly are first, for no one can cast away that which he or she does not possess.

The worship of the Gods does not exclude the worship of The One; the truth is quite the opposite, for the Gods are honourable because they are unities. This worship is the quickest and safest route to The One, perhaps the only route, for in the same way that movement in dance is that which takes the dancer from a moment of stillness to moment of stillness, and the notes in music is that which takes the listener from one silence to the next, so this worship takes the devotee to the Oneness which is behind all unities.

As Porphyry writes in his *Abstinence from Animal Foods*,[11] there is an appropriate worship for every God, including the highest:

Let us also sacrifice, but let us sacrifice in such a manner as is proper, offering different sacrifices to different powers. To that God, indeed, who is above all things, as a certain wise man says, neither fumigating nor consecrating any thing sensible. For there is nothing material, which, to an immaterial nature, is not immediately impure. Hence neither is external language adapted to him, nor that which is internal when it is defiled by any passion of the soul; but we should adore him in pure silence, and with pure conceptions concerning him. It is necessary, therefore, that, being conjoined and assimilated to him, we should offer the elevation of ourselves to Divinity as a sacred sacrifice; for thus we shall both celebrate him and procure our own salvation. In the soul's contemplation, therefore, of this divinity, unattended by the passions, the sacrifice to him receives its completion; but his progeny, the intelligible gods, are to be celebrated vocally by hymns. For to each of the gods the first fruits are to be sacrificed of what he imparts to us, and through which he nourishes and preserves us. As, therefore, the husbandman offers his first fruits from handfuls of fruits and acorns, so also we should sacrifice from beautiful conceptions concerning the gods, giving thanks for those things of which they have imparted to us the contemplation, and that, through the vision of themselves, they truly nourish us, associating with and appearing to us, and shining upon us for our salvation.

The task of the soul, the true self of each one of us, being a creature which spans the two worlds of spirit and matter, is a twofold one: to discover her unity in the highest heaven, and to animate with spiritual life the mundane.

The former is possible through the discovery of the unity of the Gods, and the latter is possible through the discovery of the goodness of the Gods.

Every level and every locality of the universe is ruled and made sacred by a God: one of the great destructive qualities of the premature monotheism of the west is the denial of this sacredness. Over and over again we see the deep spirituality of so many of the world's peoples undermined by the well-meaning but truly ignorant proselytizers of Christianity and Islam, who bring in their wake a kind of religious imperialism.[†] The local mountain, forest and river so long cherished as the habitat of the worshipped God, becomes, with the arrival of the missionary, a merely exploitable lump of geographical matter. And what is withdrawn from these locations and transferred to the two or three chosen 'holy sites,' such as Jerusalem and Mecca, actually becomes poisonous to those very sites, as too many people feel they have some vested

---

[†] I would not like the reader to think that I am against either of these religions *per se*; far from it, since they have at their heart great truths and wonderful beauties. Christianity brings with it a profound understanding of the mystery of divinity immanent within the human being, and has played a significant part in the raising of our awareness of the value of each individual - to take just two important aspects of that religion. Islam, too, has its proper contributions to make, such as an awareness of the underlying unity of all things, and all laws. If these two religions were to take their unexclusive part in the community of world religions, rather than belittle and exclude other religions, their ill-effects would be reduced and the insights they bring would be increased in power and goodness.

interest in a place in which they will never live, nor commune with the local spirit of the place. Furthermore we can see the same effect in other aspects of our lives; for example in the question of sex. The One is, of course, far beyond the duality of male and female - but if this great God of Gods is reduced in the human mind to the state of the personal and 'immediate' then it is all too easy to attribute to the highest God either masculinity or femininity. Once this happens the inevitable consequence is the loss of the sense of the sacred in the rejected sex; the evils that follow from this particular imbalance are all too obvious to require expansion here.

The ancient religion, polytheistic in expression and monotheistic in its silent centre, has only been deserted in the relatively recent past. In the future, I am sure, humankind will look upon the last two millennia as a backwater into which we have drifted, and from which it was necessary to return, taking with us the useful lessons learnt from our departure from the ways of universal humanity. In the great sweep of human history the exploration of these backwaters will play a positive part, but our return to the mainstream of progressive spiritualisation, based on the stability of true divine worship, is now becoming a matter of real urgency.

Therefore I urge the reader to recover his or her ancient heritage, the universal religion of 'God and the Gods' which, as I hope I have shown, is not only redemptive of the soul, and of the portion of the mundane world over which each individual has influence, but *is based on the greatest truths and deepest beauties known to humankind.*

This may seem an almost impossible task, since so much of our spiritual heritage has been buried over the centuries: but consider yourselves heroes and heroines and remember what seemingly impossible quests have been successfully accomplished by the unfoldment of the soul's powers and with divine help. I can finish with no finer words than those of the Golden Verses of the Pythagoreans:[12]

> Betake yourself to the work,
> Having implored the Gods, to bring it to perfection.

Notes

1. The five quotes from Homer can be found at 680a, 681e, 707a, 777a and 804a.

2. *Laws*, 658d.

3. *Phædrus* 250b.

4. *Phædrus* 244b.

5. *Euthyphro* 6a ff.

6. Plotinus, *Ennead* I, vi, 9; TTS vol. III, p. 18.

7. *On the Mysteries* V, 26.

8. See the *Works of Plato* IV, TTS vol. XII, p. 34.

9. *Theology of Plato*, II, 11, TTS vol. VIII, p. 166.

10. See for example, *Timæus* 34b - "the universe [or great world] is a happy God."

11. *Abstinence from Animal Foods*, II, 34. See page 64, *Selected Writings of Porphyry*, The Prometheus Trust, Frome 1994.

12. Verses 48 and 49.

Further reading,
and work to which references have been made.

1 Ancient myth sources

Homeric Hymns, available in many translations, for example A N Athanassakis, John Hopkins U.P., and H G Evelyn-White in the Loeb edition (volume 57).

Diodorus Siculus: Library of History, ed. C H Oldfather *et al*, Cambridge, Mass.

Hesiod's Theogony, also available in many translations, again, for example, the Loeb edition (57).

Hesiod's Works and Days, also included in the Loeb vol. 57.

Kallimachos' Hymns; I have used the Banks translation (from Bohn's Classical Library Series) but as this is out of print, I would suggest the Oxford edition, ed. Pfeiffer.

Pausanias' Guide to Greece available from Penguin Books, trans. Peter Levi; the Thomas Taylor translation will soon be available in the Thomas Taylor Series from the Prometheus Trust (see below).

The Cratylus of Plato, TTS vol. XIII (see below) also includes most of Proclus' Commentary.

Apollodorus' Library, trans. R. Hard, OUP.

The Iliad, Homer, there are numerous translations available.

The Odyssey, Homer, again, there are many translations available.

The Protagoras of Plato, TTS vol. XIII, gives some details of the Prometheus myth.

Orphic Hymns, trans. Thomas Taylor, TTS vol. V.

Agamemnon, Aeschylus; there is a good version available in a Penguin paperback, *The Orestian Trilogy*.

Oedipus at Colonus, Sophocles, available in the paperback *Three Theban Plays*.

2 Modern myth collections and commentaries
Early Greek Myth, Gantz, John Hopkins U.P.

Eleusis, C Kerenyi, Princeton U.P.

The Eleusinian and Bacchic Mysteries, Thomas Taylor, TTS vol. VII, see below for details of all Taylor's works.

Golden Age of Myth and Legend, T Bullfinch.

Classic Myth and Legend, Moncrieff.

Greek Myth, R Graves.

Dionysus, Myth and Cult, Walter F Otto. Indiana UP.

Euripides and Dionysus, R P Winnington-Ingram.

The Hero with a Thousand Faces, Joseph Campbell, Paladin.

Prometheus, Karl Kerenyi.

The Gods of the Greeks, Karl Kerenyi, Thames & Hudson.

The Heroes of the Greeks, Karl Kerenyi, Thames & Hudson.

3 Philosophical works - see also section 5.

Commentary on the Phædo of Plato, (in two volumes) Damascius and Olympiodorus, trans. Westerink, North Holland Press, 1976.

On Cult Images, Porphyry, trans. Edwin Hamilton Gifford, Clarendon Press, Oxford, 1903; at present only available on the Worldwide Web, at cosmopolis.com/texts/porphyry-on-images

Proclus, Neo-Platonic Philosophy and Science, L Siovanes, Yale UP, 1996.

4 Other works

Liddell and Scot's Greek Lexicon

The Tao Teh King of Lao Tsze, published in many translations; I have quoted from the Shrine of Wisdom edition, which is entitled *The Simple Way*.

The Shrine of Wisdom Magazine, from which I quote on occasion, was published between 1919 and 1947, by the Shrine of Wisdom, now of Fintry, Brook, Near Godalming, Surrey.

The History of the Great Light, by Huai Nan Tsze, The Shrine of Wisdom, 1960, Godalming.

The Festivals of the Athenians, H W Parke, Thames & Hudson.

5 The Thomas Taylor Series

The world's largest collection of truly Platonic writings are being made available by the Prometheus Trust; the Thomas Taylor Series will eventually extend to 34 volumes and will include all of Plato's writings (and the ancient commentaries on them), all of the extant writings of Aristotle (and commentaries), most of the extant writings of Proclus, as well as much by Plotinus, Porphyry, Iamblichus, and many others. These works have been extensively quoted throughout this book because, although the English is sometimes difficult, I am convinced that Taylor's translations come closest to the original spirit of the authors. At the time of writing, 19 volumes of the series have been published; my notes refer to this series in this style: *TTS vol. II.* The catalogue of titles so far available is:

I - *Proclus' Elements of Theology*

II - *Select Works of Porphyry*

Abstinence from Animal Food; Auxiliaries to the Perception of Intelligibles; Concerning Homer's Cave of the Nymphs; Taylor on the Wanderings of Ulysses.

III - *Collected Writings of Plotinus*

Twenty-seven treatises, being all the writings of Plotinus translated by Taylor.

IV - *Collected Writings on the Gods and the World*

Sallust On the Gods and the World; The Sentences of Demophilus; Ocellus on the Nature of the Universe; Taurus and Proclus on the Eternity of the World; Maternus on the Thema Mundi; The Emperor Julian's Orations to the Mother of Gods and to the Sovereign Sun; Synesius on Providence; Taylor's essays on the Mythology and the Theology of the Greeks.

V - *Hymns and Initiations*

The Hymns of Orpheus together with all the published hymns translated or written by Taylor; Taylor's essay on Orpheus.

VI - *The Dissertations of Maximus Tyrius*

Forty-one treatises by the middle Platonist, and an essay from Taylor - The Triumph of the Wise Man over Fortune.

VII - *Mysteries and Oracles*

A Collection of Chaldean Oracles; Essays on the Eleusinian and Bacchic Mysteries; The History of the Restoration of the Platonic Theology; An essay on A Platonic Demonstration of the Immortality of the Soul.

VIII - *The Theology of Plato*

The six books of Proclus on the Theology of Plato; to which is added a further book (by Taylor), replacing the original seventh book by Proclus, now lost. Extensive introduction and notes are also added.

IX - *The Works of Plato I*

General Introduction, Life of Plato, First Alcibiades (with almost all of Proclus' Commentary), Republic (with much of Proclus' Commentary).

X - *The Works of Plato II*

Laws, Epinomis, Timæus, Critias.

XI - *The Works of Plato III*

Parmenides (with Proclus' Commentary), Sophista, Phædrus (with the Scholia of Hermias), Greater Hippias, Banquet.

XII - *The Works of Plato IV*

Theætetus, Politicus, Minos, Apology of Socrates, Crito, Phædo (with extensive notes from the Commentaries of Olympiodorus and Damascius), Gorgias (with most of Olympiodorus' Scholia), Philebus (with additional notes from Olympiodorus), Second Alcibiades.

XIII - *The Works of Plato V*

Euthyphro, Meno, Protagoras, Theages, Laches, Lysis, Charmides, Lesser Hippias, Euthydemus, Hipparchus, Rivals, Menexenus, Clitopho, Io, Cratylus (with almost all of Proclus' Scholia), Epistles.

Index